THE WORKS OF JAMES BEATTIE

Printed and bound by
Antony Rowe Ltd., Chippenham, Wiltshire

POETICAL WORKS

James Beattie

With a new Introduction by
Roger J. Robinson

ROUTLEDGE/THOEMMES PRESS

This edition published by Routledge/Thoemmes Press, 1996

Routledge/Thoemmes Press
11 New Fetter Lane
London EC4P 4EE

The Works of James Beattie
10 Volumes : ISBN 0 415 13326 2

The Judgment of Paris (1765), *Verses Occasioned by the Death of the Revd Mr Charles Churchill* (1765), *To Mr Alexander Ross at Lochlee* (1768) are reproduced by kind permission of The Trustees of the National Library of Scotland.

© *Introduction* Roger J. Robinson, 1996

Routledge / Thoemmes Press is a joint imprint
of Routledge and Thoemmes Antiquarian Books Ltd.

British Library Cataloguing-in-Publication Data
A CIP record of this set is available from the British Library

Publisher's Note

The publisher has gone to great lengths to ensure the quality of this reprint but points out that some imperfections in the original book may be apparent.

Contents
Poetical Works

Introduction by Roger J. Robinson

Original Poems and Translations (1760)

The Judgment of Paris (1765)

Verses Occasioned by the death of the Revd Mr Charles Churchill (1765)

To Mr Alexander Ross at Lochlee (1768)

The Minstrel, with Some Other Poems (1784)

INTRODUCTION

In the catalogue of the British Library, Beattie is listed as 'BEATTIE (JAMES) *the poet*' – the same title by which he was known as a child in the parish school at Laurencekirk. This set of Beattie's works has seven volumes of prose, but only one of poetry, and the prose is substantial, not only in quantity, but in quality, interest, and in the regard and importance in which it was held by Beattie's contemporaries. Yet it was as a poet that Beattie exercised his most profound and lasting influence. Furthermore, this influence was very largely the effect of a single poem: *The Minstrel*. This poem will therefore be discussed first, though it was written last of any that appear in this volume. First, however, some general explanation of the volume's content is needed.

The Publication History of Beattie's Poetry
The choice of the editions of Beattie's poetry to include in the volume presented much greater difficulties than was the case with the prose. Many of Beattie's poems first appeared in magazines or as pamphlets. Those he liked best would then be selected to appear in collected editions. However, both the individual poems, and the canon of the collection, underwent successive revision and refinement. Each successive edition tended to be smaller than the previous one: though some new poems would be included, a greater number of old ones would be discarded; and the old ones which were retained would be substantially revised. The titles and dates of

the definitive collections are *Original Poems and Translations* (1760/1761; twenty-four poems), *Poems on Several Subjects* (1766; twelve poems, of which six were new to the collection), *Poems on Several Occasions* (1776; *The Minstrel*, plus nine other poems of which four were new to the collection), and *The Minstrel, with Some Other Poems* (1779 and 1784; no new poems included, but one omitted from the 1776 collection).

This is a much simplified bibliography of Beattie's poetry, and the subject has been a source of considerable confusion, because of the variety of forms and locations in which Beattie published his poetry, and the peculiar way in which he handled his canon. A little further explanation is therefore necessary. Three important poems were printed as pamphlets in the 1760s: *The Judgment of Paris* and *Verses Occasioned by the Death of the Revd Mr Charles Churchill* in 1765, and *To Mr Alexander Ross at Lochlee* in 1768. The first two appeared in *Poems on Several Subjects* in 1766, but were subsequently rejected from Beattie's collections; the third never appeared in his name during his life. All three pamphlets are reproduced in this set.

The two books of *The Minstrel* were also first published as quarto pamphlets: the first book in 1771, and as four subsequent pamphlet editions; the second book in 1774, and as two subsequent pamphlet editions. The first authorized edition of the two books of *The Minstrel* together was in *Poems on Several Occasions* (1776). The 1784 edition of *The Minstrel, with Some Other Poems* has been chosen for this set, because it has Beattie's final revisions, and because its text of *The Minstrel* is probably the one which was known to Wordsworth and the other Romantics.

The present volume therefore has *Original Poems and Translations*, Beattie's first book, and the one which first established his reputation as a poet; the three pamphlets; and *The Minstrel, with Some Other Poems* (1784). The last was Beattie's final definitive edition: it contained all the poems he was still prepared to acknowledge, and they were 'revised and corrected for the last time'. There were, in fact, further editions in Beattie's lifetime by his authorized publishers, in 1795, 1797 and 1799. However, they were only correct in Beattie's eyes inasmuch as they followed the text of 1784: the 1795 edition, and the earlier issue of that of 1797 did not.

Four poems appear twice in this volume: the only ones from *Original Poems and Translations* which survived into Beattie's final canon. These duplicate poems are of great interest, because they reveal how extensively Beattie revised his verse.

'The Minstrel'

In October 1795, William Wordsworth was walking on the hills near Lyme in Dorset. As he told William Mathews: 'I could hear the murmuring of the sea for three miles, of course I often stopped "listening with pleasing dread to the deep roar of the wide weltering waves". This from the Minstrel.'[1] So on that walk, the lines that immediately came into his mind were from James Beattie's *Minstrel*; of which he asked Mathews urgently terms to send him a copy, his own having gone astray.

Two years earlier, Dorothy Wordsworth had written a long letter to Jane Pollard describing her brother William's character.[2] She quoted: 'In truth he was a

---

[1] *The Letters of William and Dorothy Wordsworth, The Later Years*, edited by E. de Selincourt, 3 vols. (Oxford, 1939), vol. 3, p. 1334.

[2] *The Early Letters of William and Dorothy Wordsworth*, edited by E. de Selincourt (Oxford, 1935), p. 93.

strange and wayward wight', and said 'That verse of Beattie's *Minstrel* always reminds me of him, and indeed the whole character of Edwin [the Minstrel in the poem] resembles much what William was' [when he was seventeen].

These two quotations illustrate three of the most important characteristics of this remarkable poem: the appeal of its descriptions of nature, the attraction and fascination of the character of Edwin its protagonist, and the enthralment the poem held for the imagination of Wordsworth and the Romantics. Its influence was huge, and is still being recognized: it has even been described as the most influential poem published between *Paradise Lost* and *Lyrical Ballads*.[3] So much has been written, and rightly, on the poem's importance in the history of literature, however, that it is possible to lose sight of the revelation awaiting the new reader – that it is, in its own right, a very beautiful poem.

The Minstrel is about a boy brought up in mountainous country in Scotland, who feels called to be a poet, and about the influences on his development, particularly his response to nature. Beattie wrote this summary of it to his friend the poet Thomas Gray:

> I suppose my Hero born in a solitary and mountainous country; by trade a shepherd. His imagination is wild and romantick; but in the first part of his life he has hardly any opportunity of acquiring knowledge, except from that part of the book of nature which is open before him. The first Canto is a kind of poetical or sentimental history of this period. In the second he

---

[3] Earl A. Aldrich, 'James Beattie's *Minstrel*: Its Sources and Influence' (unpublished doctoral thesis, Harvard University, 1927), p. 286.

meets with a hermit; who...instructs Edwin (the young Minstrel) in history, philosophy, musick &c. The young man...shows a strong attachment to poetry, which the old hermit endeavours by all possible means to discourage. Edwin seems disposed to follow his advice, and abandon the muses, when an irruption of Danes or robbers (I have not as yet determined which) strips him of his little all, and obliges him through necessity to take his harp on his shoulder and go abroad into the world in the character of a Minstrel. And here the poem is to end. – The measure is the same with that of Spenser in the fairy queen.[4]

In Beattie's original plan there were a number of elements to the poem, including biographical and narrative, but because the rather far-fetched sounding third book never got written, the emphasis shifted away from the narrative toward the biographical. The theme became Edwin's poetic development; like *The Prelude*, it is a poem about the growth of a poet's mind. Furthermore, this part of the poem was not just biographical but autobiographical. Beattie wrote:

> I have made [Edwin] take pleasure in the scenes in which I took pleasure [in my younger days] and entertain sentiments similar to those, of which, even in my early youth, I had repeated experience. The scenery of a mountainous country, the ocean, the sky, thoughtfulness and retirement, and sometimes melancholy objects and ideas, had charms in my eyes, even when I was a schoolboy; and at a time that I was so

---

[4] Letter to Gray, 6 December 1769. *Correspondence of Thomas Gray*, edited by Paget Toynbee and Leonard Whibley, 3 vols. (Oxford, 1935), vol. 3, p. 1084.

far from being able to express, that I did not understand, my own feelings. (Forbes, *Life*, vol. 1, p. 207)

Edwin is gentle, innocent, strange, and rather solitary:

> Deep thought oft seem'd to fix his infant eye...
> Silent when glad; affectionate, though shy;
> And now his look was most demurely sad;
> And now he laugh'd aloud, yet none knew why.
> The neighbours stared and sigh'd, yet bless'd the lad:
> Some deem'd him wondrous wise, and some believed him mad. (Book 1, stanza 16)

> [He] roam'd at large the lonely mountain's head;
> Or, where the maze of some bewilder'd stream
> To deep untrodden groves his footsteps led,
> There would he wander wild. (Book 1, stanza 17)

He has a gentle disposition to all parts of nature, and he hates cruelty:

> His heart, from cruel sport estranged, would bleed
> To work the wo of any living thing...
> He wish'd to be the guardian, not the king,
> Tyrant far less, or traitor of the field. (Book 1, stanza 18)

Like Wordsworth in *The Prelude* and *The Excursion*, Edwin is moved by sunrises and sunsets:

> And oft he traced the uplands, to survey,
> When o'er the sky advanced the kindling dawn,
> The crimson cloud, blue main, and mountain grey,
> And lake, dim-gleaming on the smoky lawn;
> Far to the west the long long vale withdrawn,
> Where twilight loves to linger for a while;
> And now he faintly kens the bounding fawn,
> And villager abroad at early toil.

But, lo! the sun appears! and heaven, earth, ocean,
smile. (Book 1, stanza 20)

The stanza which Dorothy Wordsworth told Jane Pollard exactly described William Wordsworth as she remembered him at age seventeen shows Edwin, like Wordsworth, 'fostered alike by beauty and by fear':

In truth he was a strange and wayward wight,
Fond of each gentle, and each dreadful scene.
In darkness, and in storm, he found delight:
Nor less, than when on ocean-wave serene
The southern sun diffused his dazzling shene.
(Book 1, stanza 22)

Edwin also enjoys the sounds of the morning (Book 1, stanzas 38 and 39); he listens enraptured to the gothic stories told by the beldame at the winter fireside (Book 1, stanzas 43–52), but he most loves being out among the elements at all seasons:

Oft, when the winter-storm had ceased to rave,
He roam'd the snowy waste at even, to view
The cloud stupendous, from th' Atlantic wave
High-towering, sail along th' horizon blue...

Thence musing onward to the sounding shore
The lone enthusiast oft would take his way,
Listening with pleasing dread to the deep roar
Of the wide-weltering waves. (Book 1, stanzas 53–4)

Those were the lines Wordsworth recalled on the hills near Lyme.

A summary of Edwin's poetic growth makes him sound just like one of the Romantics:

Meanwhile, whate'er of beautiful, or new,
Sublime, or dreadful, in earth, sea, or sky,

> By chance, or search, was offer'd to his view,
> He scan'd with curious and romantic eye. (Book 1, stanza 58)

The second book of *The Minstrel*, which was published in 1774, three years after the first, is more philosophical and didactic, and recounts Edwin's instruction in history and philosophy by a hermit. Edwin achieves a balance between the world of imagination which had moved him as a child, and the world of reason presented by the hermit, but he remains devoted to poetry:

> But She, who set on fire his infant heart,
> And all his dreams, and all his wanderings shared
> And bless'd, the Muse, and her celestial art,
> Still claim th' Enthusiast's fond and first regard. (Book 2, stanza 58)

A great attraction of *The Minstrel* is in the fresh descriptions of natural scenery, and its sounds and weather and light. There is also a hint of Wordsworth's idea of the moral power of Nature, especially in the two stanzas which Thomas Gray liked the most:[5]

> O how canst thou renounce the boundless store
> Of charms which Nature to her votary yields!
> The warbling woodland, the resounding shore,
> The pomp of groves, and garniture of fields;
> All that the genial ray of morning gilds,
> And all that echoes to the song of even,
> All that the mountain's sheltering bosom shields,
> And all the dread magnificence of heaven,
> O how canst thou renounce, and hope to be forgiven!

---

[5] Letter to Beattie, March 8, 1771. *Gray Correspondence*, vol. 3, p. 1169.

These charms shall work thy soul's eternal health,
And love, and gentleness, and joy, impart. (Book 1,
stanzas 9–10)

The greatest appeal of the poem, however, was in the portrait of Edwin. Edwin was the young natural poet in the making, and other poets were moved by his communion with nature and his freedom of imagination. They were also moved by the exploration of Edwin's childhood: by the growth of a poet's mind. Individual ingredients of this mix were not new in eighteenth century poetry. Forty years before *The Minstrel*, James Thomson in *The Seasons* had described landscape and rural life, and then Mark Akenside in *The Pleasures of Imagination* had explored imaginative processes. Thomas Gray had written about childhood, somewhat pessimistically, in the *Ode on a Distant Prospect of Eton College*. But it was Beattie who brought all these themes together, and painted the development of the imagination in response to nature in a poet's childhood, and who did it in the extraordinarily appealing form of Edwin.

The Origin of 'The Minstrel'. Beattie began *The Minstrel* in 1766, and said the first hint of it had come from Thomas Percy's *Essay on the Ancient English Minstrels*, prefixed to his *Reliques of Ancient English Poetry*, published in 1765. 'There is something in the character of the Minstrel there described, which struck me and pleased me':[6] a character which was 'was not only respectable, but sacred'. Beattie was extremely well-read, and he probably drew on many other sources

---

[6] See reference 4.

for the ideas of *The Minstrel*: Spenser, and Thomson's *Castle of Indolence*, for the use of the Spenserian stanza; his teacher Thomas Blackwell (author of *An Enquiry into the Life and Writings of Homer*, 1735) for the idea of the poet in primitive society; Virgil, Thomson, and possibly 'Ossian' for the descriptions of external nature; and Rousseau's *Emile* for the innocence and education of Edwin. Many others sources could be cited, and Aldrich has reviewed the matter thoroughly. However, *The Minstrel* is not a pastiche of other people's poetic ideas; furthermore, Beattie's plan for it changed and became more original. The first outline was to include comic, narrative and sentimental components; the earliest editions of Book 1 had a trace of comedy in the opening stanzas, two of which were later removed. As Beattie says in the 'Advertisement' to the 1784 volume, the greater part of the poem was written in 1768: this probably comprised most of Book 1 from stanza 15 on, and about the first half of Book 2. These parts contain nearly all the romantic descriptions of scenery, and the exploration of Edwin's childhood and poetic development: virtually all those sections which have always exercised the greatest appeal. For those parts, his most important source was the recollection in tranquillity of his own childhood and early manhood in the landscape of the Howe of the Mearns. It is as though Beattie had a sudden burst of creative, poetic imagination in the spring and early summer of 1768. This was also the time when he wrote *To Mr Alexander Ross at Lochlee*, celebrating the natural and linguistic landscape of his childhood. The latter part of the second book of *The Minstrel*, recounting Edwin's education by the hermit was written slowly and at long intervals between 1769 and 1774; it lacks the imaginative warmth of the first book and of the earlier part of the second. This account has emphasized the romantic aspects of the poem, and the parts describing Edwin's boyhood and development, because these undoubtedly gave *The Minstrel* its greatest appeal. Such an account, however, ignores the important fact that only half the stanzas are directly about Edwin. The remaining half are equally divided between observations in the poet's own voice, and the speeches and meditations of the hermit. The poet's and the hermit's concerns are very similar: partly prayers for Edwin, or advice to him, that he should not lose his innocence, goodness, love of nature, and freedom from worldly ambition; and partly philosophical instruction, and general reflections about truth versus infidelity, and simplicity versus ambition and worldly pomp. Half the poem therefore belongs to Edwin, the young romantic, and half to Beattie, the moral philosopher. Since Edwin represents at least in part the young Beattie, the poem might be viewed as a dialogue between the young poet and his older self. The truth is probably more complex: that there was a continuing conflict in Beattie's soul between the romantic and the rationalist–moralist. For a brief period in 1768, the romantic element won.

Beattie made conflicting statements about his further intentions for the poem; but before the second book was published in 1774, he had almost certainly abandoned his plan for a third book, concerning Edwin's adventures against the invading Danes (or robbers). The idea would have been wholly incongruous with the character of the gentle, introspective poet of nature and the imagination, which he had by then created. Such was the appeal and popularity of the poem that at least three 'continuations' were published by different authors in the early nineteenth century, in which Edwin takes part

xviii *Introduction*

in improbable chivalric exploits.[7] All that any of them achieves is to show how wise Beattie was to end the poem where he did.

The Influence of 'The Minstrel'. The poem's influence was profound. The poets who were strongly affected by it included Cowper, Burns, Bowles, Samuel Rogers, Scott, Byron, Keats, Shelley, and John Clare; but above all Wordsworth. Wordsworth was first introduced to *The Minstrel* at Hawkshead School, about the age of fourteen.[8] At seventeen, when he wrote his long juvenile poem *The Vale of Esthwaite*, *The Minstrel* had got deep into his poetic make-up. There are many verbal echoes of *The Minstrel* in Wordsworth, the most important perhaps being the sea of mist in the famous Climbing of Snowdon episode of *The Prelude*.[9] The boyhood of the Wanderer or Pedlar in *The Excursion* strongly resembles Edwin's childhood, as John Wilson was the first to point out.[10] But the part of *The Ruined Cottage* or *The Excursion* which describes the boyhood of the Pedlar is also Wordsworth's first poetic autobiography, so in the young Pedlar there is a blend of the young

---

[7] William Cameron, *Poems on Several Occasions* (Edinburgh, 1813), p. 45; 'The Minstrel: a Poem in five books. The first two books by Dr Beattie; the last three by the Rev. R. Polwhele', in *The Poetical Register and Repository of Fugitive Poetry* (London, 1814) p. 48; John Herman Merivale, *Poems Original and Translated*, 2 vols. (London, 1838), vol. 1, p. 5.

[8] T. W. Thompson, *Wordsworth's Hawkshead*, edited by Robert Woof (Oxford, 1970), p. 344.

[9] Jonathan Wordsworth, *William Wordsworth: the Borders of Vision* (Oxford, 1982), p. 311.

[10] *Blackwood's Edinburgh Magazine*, vol. 44 (1838), pp. 508–23.

Edwin and the young Wordsworth. Clearly he identified himself with Edwin, a point made by Mary Moorman.[11] Beattie's influence on Wordsworth and the Romantics was explored by Earl Aldrich, and more recently has been very fully argued by Everard King, who maintains that the concept of romantic autobiography, of which *The Prelude* is the supreme example, originated in Beattie's *Minstrel*.[12] 'Romantic Spenserianism', as Kucich has shown, was also much influenced by *The Minstrel*.[13]

So much has been written of how the young writers of the Romantic period identified themselves with Edwin and were affected by *The Minstrel* that it will be sufficient to quote one less well-known, but characteristic, response. John Thelwall, 'the agitator', and friend of Wordsworth and Coleridge, described how he took Beattie's poems on one of his journeys, because

> a few passages from the minstrel would be no bad motto to our excursion... It is impossible for me ever to recall, without a sense of gratitude, the delightful sensations with which I have often perused this sublimest moralist that ever culled among the inspiring charms of nature 'The sweets that work the soul's eternal health, and Love, and Gentleness, and Joy impart!' [slightly misquoting from *The Minstrel*, Book

---

[11] Mary Moorman, *William Wordsworth: The Early Years 1770–1803* (Oxford, 1957), p. 60.

[12] Everard H. King's evidence on this subject is summarized in *James Beattie* (Boston, 1977), and particularly *James Beattie's 'The Minstrel' and the Origins of Romantic Autobiography* (Lewiston/Lampeter/Queenston, 1992).

[13] Greg Kucich, *Keats, Shelley, and Romantic Spenserianism* (Pennsylvania, 1991).

1, stanza 10]. It was one of those books, which, in my earlier and more unfortunate years, I snatched a trifle from...the common necessaries of life to procure. And I was richly repaid...

My anxious heart could not but receive some consolation, when...I traced in the youthful manners and dispositions of Edwin, the faithful delineation of my own boyish years; and beheld, as in a mirror, the reflection of those features that so evidently marked my own eccentric mind.[14]

'Original Poems and Translations'

From 1756, occasional poems by Beattie began to appear in the *Scots Magazine*. The earliest printed was the *Elegy* 'Tir'd with the busy crouds' (p. 70), which carried the date 20 February 1756. However, the translation from Lucretius, and perhaps parts of the Virgil translations, were written even earlier. In March 1759, Beattie wrote the title 'Original Poems and Translations' on the cover of a notebook, and began to transcribe his poems, making extensive revisions to the earlier versions.[15] By October 1760, the poems were ready for the press, and Beattie then wrote the Preface. Two issues of the book exist, with the imprints 'London, 1760' and 'Aberdeen, 1761'. Both, however, used identical sheets, which were all printed in Aberdeen, and both issues were published in February 1761.

This book first established Beattie's poetic reputation. He was hailed by the reviewers as 'a new acquisition to the Republic of Letters', and compared with Gray and

---

[14] John Thelwall ['Sylvanus Theophrastus'], *The Peripatetic; or, Sketches of the Heart, of Nature and Society*, 3 vols. (Southwark, 1793), vol. 1, pp. 95-7.

[15] Beattie to Aaron Lithgow, Aberdeen, 20 March 1759 (National Library of Scotland MS 2543, folios 3 and 4).

Akenside.[16] The verdicts of time, and of the older Beattie, were less kind to this collection: Beattie rejected all but four of its twenty-four pieces from his final canon, saying he would 'not rescue them from oblivion', and, it is said, destroying all copies of the book on which he could lay hands.

The poems which appealed most to the early reviewers were the two Pindaric *Odes, to Peace* and *to Hope* (whose structure he probably modelled on Gray's Odes), and *The Triumph of Melancholy*. Each has rather heavy allegory and personification, but some stanzas had a particular contemporary appeal: the lines on childhood in the *Ode to Hope* ('When first on Childhood's eager gaze/Life's varied landscape stretch'd immense around'), on the death of Brutus in *The Triumph of Melancholy*, and the final lines of the *Ode to Peace*, which were often quoted.

'Virgil has given us the pastoral poem in its most perfect state' (*Essays*, p. 110). The translations of the Virgil Pastorals (Eclogues), which close the volume, are one of Beattie's most underrated works. They were probably written in 1757–8, though an earlier date is possible. The translation, without being slavishly literal, is accurate as to meaning, clear, and melodious. It is an early manifestation of Beattie's lifelong love of Virgil: Ogilby's translation of Virgil was his first introduction to English verse, and 'if I have any true relish for the beauties of nature, I may say with truth, that it was from Virgil and from Thomson that I caught it' (Forbes, *Life*,

---

[16] *Monthly Review*, vol. 24 (1761), pp. 393–5; *Scots Magazine*, vol. 23 (1761), pp. 196–7.

vol. 2, p. 21). Beattie's introductory notes to each of the Pastorals show his early interest in the poetry of landscape, and Virgil's natural descriptions are particularly lovingly translated. Here, Beattie sometimes adds descriptive touches of his own, as at the end of the ninth Pastoral:

> And now the streams
> In slumber-soothing murmurs softly flow;
> And now the sighing breeze hath ceas'd to blow.
> (p. 178)

The sound of running water at night is a favourite poetic theme of Beattie's; it is not in Virgil's original. It is also heard in a beautiful sunset scene at the end of *The Hares*:

> Now from the western mountain's brow,
> Compast with clouds of various glow
> The sun a broader orb displays,
> And shoots aslope his ruddy rays.
> The lawn assumes a yellower green,
> And dew-drops spangle all the scene.
> The fragrant gale sighs soft along,
> The shepherd chaunts his simple song,
> With all their lays the groves resound,
> And falling waters murmur round. (p. 65)

The Hares is based on an Aesopic fable 'The Hares and Frogs', which Beattie has greatly altered and expanded. In place of some rather repulsive and mindless frogs, who dive into slime, he substitutes a frightened but attractive linnet, who eventually sings joyously from a bough. This poem deservedly survived, in a shortened form, into Beattie's final canon, though he was always critical of it, and unlike, for example, the rejected *Ode to Peace*, it had few supporters among his friends.

Among the shortest poems are two beautiful epitaphs. The one on the two drowned brothers (p. 68) commemorates a real event, and was inscribed on an actual tombstone; the other (p. 66), written when he was twenty-one, is for himself, the asterisks in the title representing 'James Beattie'. Its ending is touching and appropriate:

> Forget my frailties, thou art also frail;
> Forgive my lapses, for thyself mayst fall;
> Nor read unmov'd my artless tender tale,
> I was a friend, O man, to thee, to all.

The poem in *Original Poems and Translations* which would become the best known, but in a substantially altered form, was *Retirement, an Ode*, which is discussed below.

The 1765 Pamphlets

In 1765, Beattie published two very different poems in pamphlet form. They were reprinted in *Poems on Several Subjects* (1766), and though he subsequently rejected them both, they represent an important stage in his poetic development.

The Judgment of Paris was Beattie's longest single poem other than *The Minstrel*; it was composed over a period of eighteen months in 1763–4, and the elegant quarto form in which it was published, with a heavily moralizing four-page preface, confirms that he had considerable ambitions for it. These were disappointed: the only review was lukewarm in its approval,[17] and apparently the pamphlet did not sell well.

---

[17] *Monthly Review*, vol. 33 (1765), pp. 23–7.

Beattie's poem, as the Preface indicates, is a moral allegory. He probably used two main classical sources. The indolent and self-indulgent character of Paris, which makes 'the catastrophe probable' is taken from Homer's *Iliad*. The scenery, and the story of the Judgment, are probably drawn from Ovid's *Heroides*. However, Beattie stripped the story of its 'trifling' and 'very ridiculous' elements – there is no apple, and no explicit beauty contest. Instead, the goddesses present Paris with rival philosophies for the conduct of life. Their speeches are vastly expanded from those of Ovid, and Pallas is made to personify wisdom and virtue, whereas in Ovid she simply offers victory in war. Furthermore, Beattie insisted that his goddesses must conform to the rules of politeness and virtue: Beattie could not allow any of them to recommend vice. This required a tricky balancing act. A contemporary reviewer believed the speech of Venus contained 'though contrary to the poet's intention, the wisest arguments of any that were offered by the celestial triumvirate'; many, including Mrs Montagu, agreed. The poem is, nevertheless, skilfully constructed, and contains many attractive stanzas, particularly in the opening description, the speech of Venus, and the dramatic conclusion.

Though the poet's purpose here is entirely different from that in *The Minstrel*, *The Judgment of Paris* is remarkable for the extent to which its phraseology and ideas resemble those of *The Minstrel*. Much of Venus's speech recommends the activities and attitudes, including love of external nature, which characterize the boy Edwin in Book 1 of *The Minstrel*.

> And oft she roams the maze of wildering groves,
> Listening the unnumber'd melodies of spring:
>
> Or to the long and lonely shore retires;

What time, loose-glimmering to the lunar beam,
Faint heaves the slumberous wave, and starry fires
Gild the blue deep with many a lengthening gleam.
(pp. 29–30)

Pallas expresses some of the same concerns as those of the hermit, and also of the poet's own voice, in their meditations and their prayers for Edwin in *The Minstrel*. An oversimplified summary is that the speech of Venus looks forward to Book 1 of *The Minstrel*, while Book 2 looks back to the speech of Pallas.

Verses Occasioned by the Death of the Revd Mr Charles Churchill is a bitter satire, which is wholly unlike any other of Beattie's poems. Charles Churchill (1731–64) had achieved fame and financial success as a satirical poet in the last three years of his life. He worked with John Wilkes on the satirical newspaper *The North Briton*, whose main targets were the government of Lord Bute, and the Scots generally. Churchill's *The Prophecy of Famine* (1763) satirized the Scots and, soon after, Churchill narrowly escaped prosecution for his part in the forty-fifth number of *The North Briton*, which libelled Bute and the King. Wilkes himself fled to France, and it was while trying to visit him there that Churchill became fatally ill, dying at Boulogne on 4 November 1764.

Beattie wrote the poem in January 1765, less than three months after Churchill's death. The bitterness of his attack probably arose from a mixture of motives – loyalty to Scotland, to the Union, and to the government of the day, contempt for Churchill as a writer, and disgust that, despite being in holy orders, Churchill had a reputation for immorality. Mixed with Beattie's contempt for Churchill and Wilkes was a dislike at that time (later to be wholly reversed) of London, its manners and its morals.[18] He had visited London in 1763, and four letters to Dr James Dun[19] show his general disapproval of what he saw: 'The amusements of this town are to me all vanity and vexation of spirit...here is nothing but uproar, confusion, and perpetual alarm; here everybody labours to rid himself of thought.' There was also a bizarre, if indirect, connection between Beattie and the Wilkes–Churchill alliance: in December 1763, Beattie's mentally deranged future brother-in-law had made a possible attempt to murder Wilkes. Wilkes behaved generously to his would-be assassin, but the affair must have caused great distress to the Dun family, to whom Beattie was becoming increasingly close.[20] Beattie attacks Churchill with extraordinary rancour:

> The hireling slave of faction and of spite,
> His country's nuisance, and a Wilkes' delight;
> Alike debauch'd in body, soul, and lays...
> For ribaldry, for libels, lewdness, lies,
> For blasphemy of all the good and wise...
> For conscience, honour, slighted, spurn'd, o'er-thrown;—

---

[18] The epigraph from Juvenal on the title-page of the 1765 edition suggests that the city was one of his targets: 'nam quis iniquae tam patiens urbis, tam ferreus, ut teneat se'; 'who can be tolerant of this monstrous city, who so iron of soul as to contain himself'. This was also the epigraph to Johnson's *London: A Poem, in Imitation of the Third Satire of Juvenal*. Beattie would certainly have known Johnson's poem, which was in the first volume of Dodsley's *Collection of Poems by Several Hands* (London, 1748 and subsequent editions). The 1763 edition was in Beattie's library.

[19] *James Beattie 'The Minstrel': Some Unpublished Letters*, edited by Alexander Mackie (Aberdeen, 1908), pp. 8–21. The original letters are in Aberdeen University Library MS 30/12.

[20] R. J. Robinson, 'The madness of Mrs Beattie's family: the strange case of the "assassin" of John Wilkes', accepted for publication in *British Journal of Eighteenth-Century Studies*.

Lo, Churchill shines the minion of renown! (p. 6)

In the closing assault, Churchill is likened to Judas: the venom seems wholly uncharacteristic of Beattie, but it had a later prose echo in the attacks on Hume and the sceptical philosophers in the *Essay on Truth*: he was capable of real hatred for those who he believed endangered the principles he held sacred. There is, however, one contrasting and attractive section of the poem, where Beattie conducts a roll-call of the poets he admires: 'Is this the land that boasts a MILTON's fire?' – a passage Coleridge may have had in mind in his *Monody on the Death of Chatterton*.

Though Beattie told his friends 'I never can repent having wrote those verses', his handling of the poem suggests that he did have misgivings about it. The original pamphlet, reproduced in this volume, was anonymous. When it had become known that he was the author, he reprinted it in *Poems on Several Subjects* in 1766, but removed the name of Churchill. Subsequently, he rejected the poem from his collection. Like *The Judgment of Paris*, however, it has echoes in *The Minstrel* – in this case, in the satirical attacks on the sceptical philosophers.

'To Mr Alexander Ross at Lochlee'

Beattie's only recognized poem in Scots dialect (there are two other unpublished ones) is one of his finest. It was written on or just before 1 June 1768, in Beattie's period of exceptional poetic creativity during that late spring.

Alexander Ross (1699–1784) had since 1732 been village schoolmaster at Lochlee, a remote village forty miles south-west of Aberdeen. At some time in the 1720s, before Beattie was born, Ross was schoolmaster at Laurencekirk, where he was a friend of Beattie's father;[21] because of this, Beattie had a particular regard for Ross.

Alexander Ross's *The Fortunate Shepherdess* (whose main title became *Helenore* in the second edition) is a poem of over four thousand lines, in heroic couplets and Scots dialect. It is a vigorous pastoral narrative, of love and of skirmishes between shepherds and highland raiders, with rich descriptions of the scenery of North-East Scotland and of rural customs. It was first published in 1768, with Beattie's encouragement, and Beattie's declared object in writing the lines *To Mr Alexander Ross*, which he sent to the *Aberdeen Journal*, was to help promote its sales.

Beattie's derogatory remarks about the Scots language, and about the difficulties he believed the Scots found in writing felicitous English, are frequently quoted. Hewitt has given a more balanced appraisal of Beattie's position, arguing that though he wanted pure English (represented especially by Addison) to be the national literary standard, he also believed in literary regionalism, and in this poem was defending the dialect of the North-East as a literary medium in its own right.[22]

The poem is an affirmation of Beattie's roots in North-East Scotland; it is the language ('leed') and landscape of that area which he celebrates in two splendid stanzas:

---

[21] The main biographical sources on Alexander Ross are the *Life* by John Longmuir in Alexander Ross, *Helenore; or, The Fortunate Shepherdess: A Poem in the Broad Scotch Dialect*, edited by John Longmuir (Glasgow, 1868), pp. 30–99, and *The Scottish Works of Alexander Ross, M.A.*, edited by Margaret Wattie (Edinburgh and London, 1938), pp. ix–xxv.

[22] David Hewitt, 'James Beattie and the Languages of Scotland', in *Aberdeen and the Enlightenment*, edited by Jennifer J. Carter and Joan H. Pittock (Aberdeen, 1987), pp. 251–60.

> Our countra' leed is far frae barren,
> It's even right pithy and aulfarren,
> Oursells are neiper-like, I warran,
>   For sense and smergh,
> In kittle times, whan faes are yarring,
>   We're no thought ergh.
>
> O bonny are our greensward hows,
> Where through the birks the burny rows,
> And the bee bums, and the ox lows,
>   And saft winds rusle,
> And shepherd-lads on sunny knows,
>   Blaw the blyth fusle.

Beattie's letters show an ambiguous attitude concerning both the Scots dialect and this poem. He acknowledged its authorship to some of his friends, but never publicly. Nevertheless, it must have become quite widely known that he had written it: in 1788 Burns, who greatly admired it, remarked "Tis a poem of Beattie's in the Scottish dialect'.[23]

'The Minstrel with Some Other Poems' (1784), and Beattie's Poetic Revisions

As already explained, the 1784 volume contains Beattie's final version of *The Minstrel*, together with the eight other poems, which were the only ones he would continue to acknowledge. Four of these – *Retirement*, *Elegy*, *Ode to Hope*, and *The Hares* – had been printed in *Original Poems and Translations* in 1761. The new versions show how extensively Beattie revised the small number of early poems which he still allowed into his

---

[23] *The Letters of Robert Burns*, edited by J. De Lancey Ferguson and G. Ross Roy, 2nd ed., 2 vols. (Oxford, 1985), vol. 1, p. 256.

collection. *The Hares*, for example, has lost 86 of its original 328 lines, and revisions have been made in a further 104 lines.

Beattie explained the reasons for his rejections and revisions to Mrs Montagu in 1778:[24]

> The truth is, that my notions of good writing have undergone a considerable change within these twelve years... We who pass all our early youth in Scotland...are obliged to study [English] as a dead language, and without the assistance of a master. Hence in our first attempts to write it we are very apt to imitate bad models. My admiration of Thomson's poetry and sentiments, and the intoxication produced by the melancholy strains of Young, made me admire also the style and the composition of those authors; which... is very unclassical, at least in the Seasons and Night-thoughts. This, I believe, will in part account for some of the miscarriages of my youth... When I had...grown more *intimately* acquainted with the most elegant Classick authors, my ideas of composition became different; I did not apprehend a poetical image with more vivacity, nor feel a just or pathetick sentiment with more energy; but in perspicuity, and simplicity, in the arrangement of parts, and in their subserviency to one determinate purpose, I began to discover charms which I had never attended to before. All this I have endeavoured to express in one of the stanza's of the Minstrel...

---

[24] Beattie to Mrs Montagu, Aberdeen, 20 April 1778 (Aberdeen University Library MS 30/1/136). Quoted in Margaret Forbes, *Beattie and his Friends* (London, 1904; reprinted Thoemmes Press, Bristol, 1990), p. 143.

> Of late with cumbersome though pompous show
> Edwin would oft his flowery rhyme deface,
> Through ardour to adorn; but Nature now
> To his experienced eye a modest grace
> Presents, where Ornament the second place
> Holds, to intrinsick worth and just design
> Subservient still. Simplicity apace
> Tempers his rage: he owns her charm divine,
> And clears th' ambiguous phrase and lops th' unwieldy line.

There is still much to be cleared and lopped in those few poems which I have lately had the face to acknowledge.

The stanza of *The Minstrel* which he quotes (Book 2, stanza 59) was probably written early in 1774. It echoes Horace's *Ars Poetica*, advising the wise man to prune pretentious ornament, clarify the ambiguous phrase, and censure lifeless or harsh lines.

So Beattie says that his rejection of his earlier poems had nothing to do with ideas or content – he did not apprehend a poetical image with more vivacity, nor feel a just or pathetick sentiment with more energy – but with style. Good style and composition, he believes, are imitative, and require attention to the best models, meaning the classics. So here, he is not anticipating the Romantics as he appeared to be doing in 1768 in the first book of *The Minstrel*, but looking backward to the Augustans.

'Retirement' and 'The Hermit': Two Notable Minor Poems

The best known of Beattie's short poems, both of which appeared frequently in anthologies, were *Retirement* and *The Hermit*. Both were originally written as songs, both were radically revised between their first published and their final versions, and both have been described as early Romantic poems.[25]

One stanza of *Retirement* was particularly celebrated, Wordsworth being especially fond of it:

> Thy shades, thy silence, now be mine,
> Thy charms my only theme;
> My haunt the hollow cliff, whose pine
> Waves o'er the gloomy stream,
> Whence the scared owl on pinions grey
> Breaks from the rustling boughs,
> And down the lone vale sails away
> To more profound repose.

Tradition associated the poem, and this stanza in particular, with a glen at Fordoun, where Beattie is said to have written much of his early poetry (Forbes, *Life*, vol. 1, p. 20). However, the 'owl' stanza was not in the earliest version; it was added with three other stanzas in *Poems on Several Subjects* in 1766; further revisions were made in 1776, producing the familiar version just quoted, which appears here in the 1784 volume (p. 67). Comparison with the version in *Original Poems and Translations* shows that *Retirement* had become an entirely different poem. In 1784, however, Beattie added the wholly misleading date '1758' to the title, suggesting that the well-known version printed in 1784 dates from Beattie's Fordoun period. In fact, it is doubtful if any of the poem was written at Fordoun: it is certain that the 'owl' stanza was not. *Retirement* was not a description of immediate experience; it was a 'recollection in

---

[25] E. H. King, 'James Beattie's *Retirement* and *The Hermit*: Two Early Romantic Poems', *South Atlantic Quarterly*, vol. 72 (1973), pp. 574–86.

Introduction xxxiii

tranquillity' of a scene and a state of mind Beattie had enjoyed many years ago. It is appropriate that Wordsworth should have held it in such affection.

The Hermit was probably even better known than *Retirement*; it appeared in anthologies of religious as well as general verse, and it was set to music by Giordani. Johnson wept over it: Jane Austen quoted it to her sister.[26] However, like *Retirement*, its well-known version is radically different from the one originally published (in the *Edinburgh Magazine and Review* in 1773). That version ended with the lines 'But when shall Spring visit the mouldering urn!/O when shall it dawn on the night of the grave'. It was therefore a lament for mortality. Beattie came under strong pressure from several friends to give it a more Christian message; in 1776, he added the final two stanzas as they appear in the 1784 volume here. It has become a hymn to the resurrection: 'And darkness and doubt are now flying away...And Beauty immortal awakes from the tomb.'

Conclusion
One of the less well-known stanzas of *The Minstrel* contains one of the most impressive and romantic images of the whole poem. It is based on Johannes Schefferus's *History of Lapland*, a seventeenth-century travel book originally written in Latin. The 1704 English translation was in Beattie's library, and from this four-hundred-page volume he plucked – in the way Coleridge plucked images or ideas from Bartram's travels or Priestley's *Optics* – two sentences:

---

[26] *Boswell's Life of Johnson*, edited by George Birkbeck Hill, revised by L. F. Powell, 6 vols. (Oxford, 1934–50), vol. 4, p. 186; *Jane Austen's Letters to her Sister Cassandra and Others*, edited by R. W. Chapman, 2nd ed. (Oxford, 1952), p. 331.

> Spring and Autumn are hardly known to the Laplanders. About the time the sun enters Cancer, their fields, which a week before were covered with snow, appear on a sudden full of grass and flowers.

Beattie used this as a simile for the bursting out of Edwin's poetic genius:

> Thus on the chill Lapponian's dreary land,
> For many a long month lost in snow profound,
> When Sol from Cancer sends the season bland,
> And in their northern cave the storms are bound;
> From silent mountains, straight, with startling sound,
> Torrents are hurl'd; green hills emerge; and lo,
> The trees with foliage, cliffs with flowers are crown'd;
> Pure rills through vales of verdure warbling go;
> And wonder, love, and joy, the peasant's heart o'erflow. (Book 1, stanza 59)

There has been a tendency to regard the poetry Beattie wrote before *The Minstrel* as though it came from 'the chill Lapponian's dreary land'. It is certainly true that, in the spring of 1768, something remarkable like the Lapland Spring was happening in Beattie's poetic imagination, which produced the finest parts of *The Minstrel*, and the lines to Alexander Ross. Nevertheless, this volume may persuade some readers that other parts of Beattie's verse deserve more regard than they have been given. *Retirement* and *The Hermit* have always rightly had admirers, but there are also rewards to be found in, for example, the Virgil translations, *The Judgment of Paris*, and the short epitaphs in *Original Poems and Translations*.

Roger J. Robinson
University of Aberdeen, 1996

ORIGINAL POEMS

AND

TRANSLATIONS.

By *JAMES BEATTIE*, A. M.

L O N D O N:

Printed; and sold by A. MILLAR in *The Strand.*
M DCC LX.

TO

THE RIGHT HONOURABLE

JAMES

EARL OF ERROLL,

LORD HIGH CONSTABLE OF SCOTLAND,

ETC. ETC. ETC.

THE FOLLOWING

POEMS AND TRANSLATIONS,

IN TESTIMONY

OF THE UTMOST ESTEEM AND GRATITUDE,

ARE

MOST RESPECTFULLY

INSCRIBED

BY

HIS LORDSHIP's

MOST OBLIGED

MOST OBEDIENT

AND MOST HUMBLE SERVANT

J. BEATTIE.

THE

PREFACE.

FEW writers are qualified to form a proper judgment of their own talents. Their opinions on this subject, whether influenced by diffidence or by vanity, are for the most part equally remote from truth. If any there be, who can with certainty anticipate the sentiments of the Public with regard to their own compositions, they must be such as are thoroughly acquainted with mankind, as well as with the propensity and the force of their own genius. But it is impossible that one, who has not experimentally proved

Quid ferre recusent,
Quid valeant humeri, *

should be able to judge for himself, either in the choice or the execution of his subject. If he wishes to have his judgment regulated in this matter, he must appeal to the Public Suffrage, which, however it may for a time be rendered ineffectual by prejudice or partial favour, will at last determine his real character.

The Author of the following little Poems hopes, that this to the goodnatured Reader will apologize for his rashness (if it shall be deemed rashness) in venturing abroad into the public view. He would not wish to labour in an hopeless pursuit; nor is he one of those who have determined (as Butler says),

In spite
Of nature and their stars to write;

* Hor. Epist. ad Pison.

the sentiments of the Public he will regard, whether they suggest hints for writing better, or cautions against writing at all.

Each of the pieces that compose this small miscellany has been read and approved by several persons of unquestionable taste, whose judgment was capable of no other bias than that amiable one, the partiality of friendship. This the Author chooses to mention; because he would not be thought to have engaged in this publication entirely in compliance with the suggestions of his own vanity: and he is afraid to urge *the request of friends* as an excuse for his appearing in his present character; this plea having been so often abused, that it is become even ridiculous.

The Public is already acquainted with several Translations of Virgil's Pastorals. Mr. Dryden's translations will be admired, as long as the English language is understood, for that fluent and graceful energy of expression, which distinguishes all the writings of that Great Poet. In his compositions, even in those which have been censured as inaccurate, we are charmed with

> * *Thoughts that breathe, and words that burn;*

and if we find any thing blameable, we are inclined to impute it, not to any defect in his own genius or taste, but to the depravity of the age in which it was his misfortune to live.

The translation of Virgil published some years ago by the learned and ingenious Mr. Joseph Warton did not come into my hands till long after what is now offered to the Public was finished. That it was well received, even after Mr. Dryden's, is a sufficient proof of its merit.

The perusal of these two masterly versions might have effectually discouraged

---

* Gray's Odes.

the publication of the following, had I ever intended it as a rival to either of the others. But as I difclaim this intention, and would wifh to be thought only an humble Copier of Virgil, I hope the prefent tranflation will be pardoned, if in a few particular inftances it be found to have fet any of the beauties of the admired Original in a more confpicuous point of view to the Englifh Reader. Nor let it be afcribed to arrogance or vanity, that I prefume to think this poffible, notwithftanding what has been fo well performed by the Great Mafters juft mentioned. In copying a painting of Raphael, an Engraver of an inferior clafs may give expreffion to a particular lineament more fuccefsfully than even Strange himfelf. A minute Obferver will fometimes attend to a little circumftance, which an enlarged imagination capable of conceiving and exhibiting the full idea may overlook. The eye is not wholly fatisfied with contemplating a piece of fculpture from the moft advantageous ftation: by changing the ftation it enjoys the satisfaction not only of viewing the same attitude in a variety of lights, but of catching the expression of some particular muscle or feature not discernible from the former point of view. It is perhaps some such consideration as this, that hath induced those, who are indulgent to my performances, to advise the publishing of this translation; which was written at a very early time of life, when solitude left the mind at liberty to pursue, without any fixed design, such amusements as gratified the present hour.

THE version from LUCRETIUS was written at the particular desire of a Friend, whose commands the Translator hath reason to honour.

N. B. The versions of the fourth, fifth, and tenth pastorals, as they are printed in former miscellaneous collections, were copied from unfinished draughts, and swarm with typographical errors, some of which are so gross that they totally pervert the sense.

THE CONTENTS.

	Page.
Ode to PEACE.	1
RETIREMENT, an Ode.	11
Ode to HOPE.	15
The Triumph of MELANCHOLY.	23
An Elegy occasioned by the death of a LADY.	40
The HARES, a Fable.	47
Epitaph.	66
Epitaph on TWO BROTHERS.	68
Elegy.	70
Song in Imitation of SHAKESPEAR.	74
ANACREON Ode 22 translated.	76
Invocation to VENUS, from LUCRETIUS, translated.	77
HORACE Book II. Ode 10. translated.	82
HORACE Book III. Ode 13. translated.	84

CONTENTS.

THE PASTORALS OF VIRGIL translated.	87
The first Pastoral.	89
The second Pastoral.	99
The third Pastoral.	107
The fourth Pastoral.	122
The fifth Pastoral.	130
The sixth Pastoral.	141
The seventh Pastoral.	150
The eighth Pastoral.	159
The ninth Pastoral.	171
The tenth Pastoral.	183

ODE TO PEACE.

I. 1.

PEACE, heaven-descended maid! whose powerful voice
From antient darkness call'd the morn,
Of jarring elements compos'd the noise;
When Chaos from his old dominion torn,
With all his bellowing throng,
Far, far was hurl'd the void abyss along;
And all the bright Angelic Choir
To loftiest raptures tuned the heavenly lyre,
Pour'd in loud symphony th' impetuous strain:

A

And every fiery orb and planet sung,
And wide through Night's dark desolate domain
Rebounding long and deep the lays triumphant
   rung.

I. 2.

Oh whither art thou fled, Saturnian Reign!
Roll round again, majestic Years!
To break fell Tyranny's corroding chain,
From Woe's wan cheek to wipe the bitter tears,
Ye Years, again roll round!
Hark! from afar what loud tumultuous sound,
While echoes sweep the winding vales,
Swells full along the plains, and loads the gales!
Murder deep-rous'd, with the wild whirlwind's haste
And roar of tempest, from her cavern springs,
Her tangled serpents girds around her waist,
Smiles ghastly-stern, and shakes her gore-distilling
   wings.

I. 3.

Fierce up the yielding skies
The shouts redoubling rife:
Earth shudders at the dreadful sound,
And all is listening trembling round.
Torrents, that from yon promontory's head
Dash'd furious down in desperate cascade,
Heard from afar amid the lonely night
That oft have led the wanderer right,
Are silent at the noise.
The mighty ocean's more majestic voice
Drown'd in superiour din is heard no more;
The surge in silence sweeps along the foamy shore.

II. 1.

The bloody banner streaming in the air
Seen on yon sky-mix'd mountain's brow,
The mingling multitudes, the madding car
Pouring impetuous on the plain below,

War's dreadful Lord proclaim.

Bursts out by frequent fits th' expansive flame.

Whirl'd in tempestuous eddies flies

The surging smoke o'er all the darken'd skies.

The chearful face of heaven no more is seen,

Fades the Morn's vivid blush to deadly pale,

The bat flits transient o'er the dusky green,

Night's shrieking birds along the sullen twilight sail.

II. 2.

Involv'd in fire-streak'd gloom the car comes on.

The mangled steeds grim Terror guides.

His forehead writh'd to a relentless frown,

Aloft the angry Power of battles rides:

Grasp'd in his mighty hand

A mace tremendous desolates the land;

Thunders the turret down the steep,

The mountain shrinks before its wasteful sweep:

Chill horror the diffolving limbs invades

Smit by the blafting lightning of his eyes,

A bloated palenefs Beauty's bloom o'erfpreads,

Fades every flowery field, and every verdure dies.

II. 3.

How ftartled Phrenzy ftares,

Briftling her ragged hairs!

Revenge the gory fragment gnaws;

See, with her griping vulture-claws

Imprinted deep, fhe rends the opening wound!

Hatred her torch blue-ftreaming toffes round;

The fhrieks of agony, and clang of arms

Re-echo to the fierce alarms

Her trump terrific blows.

Difparting from behind the clouds difclofe

Of kingly gefture a gigantic form,

That with his fcourge fublime directs the whirling ftorm.

III. 1.

Ambition, outside fair! within more foul
Than fellest fiend from Tartarus sprung,
In caverns hatch'd, where the fierce torrents roll
Of Phlegethon, the burning banks along,
Yon naked waste survey:
Where late was heard the flute's mellifluous lay;
Where late the rosy-bosom'd Hours
In loose array danced lightly o'er the flowers;
Where late the shepherd told his tender tale;
And wak'd by the soft-murmuring breeze of morn
The voice of chearful Labour fill'd the dale;
And dove-eyed Plenty smil'd, and wav'd her liberal
horn.

III. 2.

Yon ruins sable from the wasting flame
But mark the once-resplendent dome;
The frequent corse obstructs the sullen stream,

And ghosts glare horrid from the sylvan gloom.

How sadly-silent all!

Save where outstretch'd beneath yon hanging wall

Pale Famine moans with feeble breath,

And Torture yells, and grinds her bloody teeth—

Though vain the muse, and every melting lay,

To touch thy heart, unconscious of remorse!

Know, monster, know, thy hour is on the way,

I see, I see the Years begin their mighty course.

III. 3.

What scenes of glory rise

Before my dazzled eyes!

Young Zephyrs wave their wanton wings,

And melody celestial rings:

Along the lillied lawn the nymphs advance

Flush'd with Love's bloom, and range the sprightly
    dance:

The gladsome shepherds on the mountain-side

Array'd in all their rural pride
Exalt the festive note,
Inviting Echo from her inmost grot—
But ah! the landscape glows with fainter light,
It darkens, swims, and flies for ever from my sight.

IV. 1.

Illusions vain! Can sacred PEACE reside,
Where sordid gold the breast alarms,
Where cruelty inflames the eye of Pride,
And Grandeur wantons in soft Pleasure's arms!
Ambition! these are thine:
These from the soul erase the form divine;
These quench the animating fire,
That warms the bosom with sublime desire.
Thence the relentless heart forgets to feel,
Hate rides tremendous on th' o'erwhelming brow,
And midnight-Rancour grasps the cruel steel,
Blaze the funereal flames, and sound the shrieks of
Woe.

IV. 2.

From Albion fled, thy once-belov'd retreat,

What region brightens in thy smile,

Creative PEACE, and underneath thy feet

Sees sudden flowers adorn the rugged soil?

In bleak Siberia blows

Wak'd by thy genial breath the balmy rose?

Wav'd over by thy magic wand

Does life inform fell Lybia's burning sand?

Or does some isle thy parting flight detain,

Where roves the Indian through primeval shades;

Haunts the pure pleasures of the woodland reign,

And led by Reason's ray the path of Nature treads?

IV 3.

On Cuba's utmost steep *

Far leaning o'er the deep

---

* This alludes to the discovery of America by the Spaniards under Columbus. These ravagers are said to have made their first descent on the islands in the gulph of Florida, of which Cuba is one.

'The Goddess' pensive form was seen.
Her robe of Nature's varied green
Wav'd on the gale; grief dim'd her radiant eyes,
Her swelling bosom heav'd with boding sighs:
She eyed the main; where, gaining on the view,
Emerging from th' etherial blue,
Midst the dread pomp of war
Gleam'd the Iberian streamer from afar.
She saw; and on refulgent pinions born
Slow wing'd her way sublime, and mingled with
the morn.

RETIREMENT,

AN ODE.

SHOOK from the Evening's fragrant wings
    When dews impearl the grove,
And round the liſtening valley rings
The languid voice of Love;
Laid on a daiſy-ſprinkled green,
Beſide a plaintive ſtream,
A meek-eyed Youth of ſerious mein
Indulged this ſolemn theme.

Ye cliffs, in savage grandeur pil'd
High o'er the darkening dale!
Ye groves! along whose windings wild
Soft-steals the murmuring gale;
Where oft lone Melancholy strays,
By wilder'd Fancy led,
What time the wan moon's yellow rays
Stream through the chequer'd shade.

To you, ye wastes, whose artless charms
Ne'er drew Ambition's eye,
Scap'd the tumultuous world's alarms
To your retreats I fly.
Deep in your most sequester'd bower
Let me at last recline,
Where Solitude, meek modest Power,
Leans on her ivy'd shrine.

How shall I woo thee, matchless Fair!
Thy envy'd smile how win!
Thy smile, that smooths the brow of Care,
And stills each storm within!
O wilt thou to thy favourite grove
Thine ardent votary bring,
And bless his hours, and bid them move
Serene on silent wing.

There while to thee glad Nature pours
Her gently-warbling song,
And Zephyr from the waste of flowers
Wafts sweet perfumes along;
Let no rude sound invade from far,
No vagrant foot be nigh,
No ray from Grandeur's gilded car
Flash on thy startled eye.

For me, no more the path invites
Ambition loves to tread;
No more I climb life's panting heights,
By guileful Hope misled:
Leaps my fond fluttering heart no more
To Joy's enlivening lays—
Soon are the glittering moments o'er,
Soon each gay form decays.

ODE

TO HOPE.

I. 1.

O THOU that glad'ſt the penſive breaſt;
    More than Aurora's ſmile the pilgrim lorn
    Left all night long to mourn
Amidſt the horrors of the dreary waſte;
Where ſavage howls, as intermits the ſtorm,
Wide o'er the wilderneſs reſound from far,
And croſs the gloom darts many a griſly form,
And fire-eyed viſages horrific ſtare;

Hail, Goddess, friend of human race!
Hail! for thou oft thy suppliant's vow hast heard,
And oft with smiles indulgent chear'd
His doubting soul to peace.

I. 2.

Smit by thy rapture-beaming eye
Deep-flashing through the midnight of their mind,
The sable bands, combin'd
Where Fear's black banner bloats the troublous sky,
Appal'd retire: Suspicion hides her head,
Nor dares th' obliquely-glaring eye to raise;
Despair with gorgon-figur'd veil o'erspread
Speeds to Cocytus' shriek-resounding maze;
Lo, startled at the heavenly ray
With haste unwonted Indolence upsprings,
And heaving lifts her leaden wings,
And sullen glides away:

I. 3.

Ten thousand forms by pining Fancy view'd
Dissolve.   Above the sparkling flood
When Phœbus rears his awful brow,
From lengthening lawn and valley low
The troops of fen-nurst mists retire;
Along the plain the joyous swain
Eyes the green villages again,
And gold-illumin'd spire;
While on the sky's soft billows born
Floats the loose lays jovial measure;
And light along the fairy Pleasure,
Her green robes glittering to the morn,
Wantons on silken wing; and goblins all
Shrink to the deep dark vault, or hoary hall,
Or westward with impetuous flight
Shoot to the desart realms of their cogenial Night.

II. 1.

When first on Childhood's eager gaze
Life's varied landscape stretch'd immense around
Starts out of night profound,
Thy voice incites to tempt the wildering maze.
Fond he surveys thy mild maternal face,
His bashful eye still kindling as he views,
And, while thy lenient arm supports his pace,
With beating heart the upland path pursues;
The path, that leads, where, high uphung,
Seen far remote, Youth's gorgeous trophies, gay
In Fancy's vivid rainbow-ray,
Allure the eager throng.

II. 2.

Pursue thy pleasurable way,
Safe in the guidance of thy heavenly guard;
While melting airs are heard,
And soft-eyed Cherub-forms around thee play;

Simplicity, with careless flowers array'd,
Prattling amusive in his accent meek;
And Modesty, half turning as afraid,
The smile just dimpling on his glowing cheek;
Contentment pours the gentle strain;
While circled with an orb of wavy light
Fair Innocence with fearless flight
Leads on the jocund train.

II. 3.

Frail man, how various is thy lot below!
To-day, though gales propitious blow,
Though Peace soft-gliding down the sky
Bring Love along and Harmony,
Tomorrow the gay scene deforms;
Then all around, the thunder's found
Rolls rattling on through heaven's profound,
And down rush all the storms.
Ye Days, that choicest influence shed,

When gay Childhood ever sprightly
O'er flowery regions sported lightly,
Whither, ah whither are ye fled!
Ye Cherub-train, that brought him on his way,
O leave him not midst tumult and dismay;
For now Youth's eminence he gains,
But what a weary length of lingering woe remains!

III. 1.

They shrink, they vanish into air—
Now Slander taints with pestilence the gale;
And mingling cries assail,
The wail of Woe, and scream of mad Despair.
Lo, wizard Envy from his serpent-eye
Darts quick destruction in each baleful glance;
Pride smiling stern, and yellow Jealousy,
Frowning Disdain, and haggard Hate advance:
Behold, amid the dire array,
Pale, wither'd Care his giant-stature rears,

And lo, his iron hand prepares
To grasp its feeble prey.

III. 2.

Oh who shall guard bewilder'd Youth
Safe from the fierce assaults of hostile rage?
Such wars can Virtue wage,
Virtue, that bears the sacred shield of Truth?
Ah no.   On Infamy's victorious spear
Fair Virtue's spoils are oft in triumph born,
While by Adversity's decree severe
Unwept unheard the Captive wails forlorn,
Defac'd with many a cruel scar.
Ill-fated Youth, then whither wilt thou fly?
No friend, no shelter now is nigh,
And onward rolls the war.

III. 3.

But whence the sudden beam that shoots along!
Why shrink aghast the hostile throng!

Lo, from amidst Affliction's night
HOPE bursts all radiant on the sight:
Her words the troubled bosom soothe.
" Why thus dismay'd? Though foes invade,
" Hope ne'er is wanting to their aid,
" Who tread the path of Truth.
" 'Tis I, who smooth the rugged way;
" I, who close the eyes of Sorrow,
" And with glad visions of tomorrow
" Repair the weary soul's decay.
" When Death's cold touch thrills to the freezing
heart,
" Dreams of heaven's opening glories I impart,
" Till the free'd spirit springs on high
" In rapture too severe for weak Mortality".

THE TRIUMPH

OF

MELANCHOLY.

MEMORY, be ſtill! why throng upon the thought
Theſe ſcenes deep-ſtain'd with Sorrow's ſable dye?
Haſt thou in ſtore no joy-illumin'd draught,
To chear bewilder'd Fancy's tearful eye?

Yes—from afar a landſcape ſeems to riſe
Deckt gorgeous by the laviſh hand of Spring;

Thin gilded clouds float light along the skies,
And laughing Loves disport on fluttering wing.

How blest the Youth in yonder valley laid!
Soft smiles in every conscious feature play,
While to the gale low-murmuring through the glade
He tempers sweet his sprightly-warbling lay.

Hail Innocence! whose bosom all serene
Feels not fierce Passion's raving tempest roll!
Oh ne'er may Care distract that placid mien!
Oh ne'er may Doubt's dark shades o'erwhelm thy soul!

Vain wish! for lo, in gay attire conceal'd
Yonder she comes! the heart-enflaming fiend!

(Will no kind Power the helpless stripling shield!)
Swift to her destin'd prey see Passion bend!

Oh smile accurst to hide the worst designs!
Now with blithe eye she wooes him to be blest,
While round her arm unseen a serpent twines—
And lo, she hurls it hissing at his breast!

And, instant, lo, his dizzy eyeball swims
Ghastly, and reddening darts a threatful glare;
Pain with strong grasp distorts his writhing limbs,
And Fear's cold hand erects his bristling hair!

Is this, O Life, is this thy boasted prime!
And does thy spring no happier prospect yield!
Why gilds the vernal sun thy gaudy clime,
When nipping mildews waste the flowery field!

D

How Memory pains! Let some gay theme beguile
The musing mind, and sooth to soft delight.
Ye images of woe, no more recoil;
Be life's past scenes wrapt in oblivious night.

Now when fierce Winter arm'd with wasteful
power
Heaves the wild deep that thunders from afar,
How sweet to sit in this sequester'd bower,
To hear, and but to hear, the mingling war!

Ambition here displays no gilded toy
That tempts on desperate wing the soul to rise,
Nor Pleasure's flower-embroider'd paths decoy,
Nor Anguish lurks in Grandeur's gay disguise.

Oft has Contentment chear'd this lone abode
With the mild languish of her smiling eye;

Here Health has oft in blushing beauty glow'd,
While loose-robed Quiet stood enamour'd by.

Even the storm lulls to more profound repose:
The storm these humble walls assails in vain;
Screen'd is the lily when the whirlwind blows,
While the oak's stately ruin strows the plain.

Blow on, ye winds! Thine, Winter, be the skies,
Roll the old ocean, and the vales lay waste:
Nature thy momentary rage defies;
To her relief the gentler Seasons haste.

Throned in her emerald-car see Spring appear!
(As Fancy wills the landscape starts to view)
Her emerald-car the youthful *Zephyrs* bear,
Fanning her bosom with their pinions blue.

Around the jocund Hours are fluttering seen;
And lo, her rod the rose-lip'd Power extends!
And lo, the lawns are deckt in living green,
And Beauty's bright-eyed train from heaven descends!

Haste, happy Days, and make All Nature glad——
But will All Nature joy at your return?
Say, can ye chear pale Sickness' gloomy bed,
Or dry the tears that bathe th' untimely urn?

Will ye one transient ray of gladness dart
Cross the dark cell where hopeless Slavery lies?
To ease tir'd Disappointment's bleeding heart
Will all your stores of softening balm suffice?

When fell Oppression in his harpy-fangs
From Want's weak grasp the last sad morsel bears,

Can ye allay the heart-wrung parent's pangs,
Whose famish'd child craves help with fruitless tears?

For ah! thy reign, Oppression, is not past.
Who from the shivering limbs the vestment rends?
Who lays the once-rejoicing village waste,
Bursting the tyes of lovers and of friends?

O ye, to Pleasure who resign the day,
As loose in Luxury's clasping arms you lye,
O yet let pity in your breast bear sway,
And learn to melt at Misery's moving cry.

But hopest thou, Muse, vainglorious as thou art,
With the weak impulse of thy humble strain,
Hopest thou to soften Pride's obdurate heart,
When ERROLL's bright example shines in vain?

Then cease the theme. Turn, Fancy, turn thine eye,
Thy weeping eye, nor further urge thy flight;
Thy haunts alas no gleams of joy supply,
Or transient gleams, that flash, and sink in night.

Yet fain the mind its anguish would forego—
Spread then, Historic Muse, thy pictur'd scroll;
Bid thy great scenes in all their splendor glow,
And swell to thought sublime th' exalted soul.

What mingling pomps rush boundless on the gaze!
What gallant navies ride the heaving deep!
What glittering towns their cloud-wrapt turrets raise!
What bulwarks frown horrific o'er the steep!

Bristling with spears, and bright with burnish'd
    shields,
Th' embattled legions stretch their long array;
Discord's red torch, as fierce she scours the fields,
With bloody tincture stains the face of day.

And now the hosts in silence wait the sign.
How keen their looks whom Liberty inspires!
Quick as the goddess darts along the line,
Each breast impatient burns with noble fires.

Her form how graceful! In her lofty mien
The smiles of Love stern Wisdom's frown controul;
Her fearless eye, determin'd though serene,
Speaks the great purpose, and th' unconquer'd
    soul.

Mark, where Ambition leads the adverse band,
Each feature fierce and haggard, as with pain!

With menace loud he cries, while from his hand
He vainly strives to wipe the crimson stain.

Lo, at his call, impetuous as the storms,
Headlong to deeds of death the hosts are driven;
Hatred to madness wrought each face deforms,
Mounts the black whirlwind, and involves the heaven.

Now, Virtue, now thy powerful succour lend,
Shield them for Liberty who dare to die—
Ah Liberty! will none thy cause befriend!
Are these thy sons, thy generous sons that fly!

Not Virtue's self, when Heaven its aid denies,
Can brace the loosen'd nerves, or warm the heart;
Not Virtue's self can still the burst of sighs,
When festers in the soul Misfortune's dart.

See, where by heaven-bred terror all dismay'd
The scattering legions pour along the plain.
Ambition's car with bloody spoils array'd
Hews its broad way, as Vengeance guides the rein.

But who is he, that, * by yon lonely brook
With woods o'erhung and precipices rude,
Abandon'd lies, and with undaunted look
Sees streaming from his breast the purple flood?

Ah BRUTUS! ever thine be Virtue's tear!
Lo, his dim eyes to Liberty he turns,
As scarce-supported on her broken spear
O'er her expiring son the Goddess mourns.

---

* " By yon lonely brook With woods o'erhung and precipices
" rude "—Such, according to the description given by Plutarch,
was the scene of Brutus's death.

Loose to the wind her azure mantle flies,
From her dishevel'd locks she rends the plume;
No lustre lightens in her weeping eyes,
And on her tear-stain'd cheek no roses bloom.

Meanwhile the world, Ambition, owns thy sway,
Fame's loudest trumpet labours in thy praise,
For thee the Muse awakes her sweetest lay,
And Flattery bids for thee her altars blaze.

Nor in life's lofty bustling sphere alone,
The sphere where monarchs and where heroes toil,
Sink Virtue's sons beneath Misfortune's frown,
While Guilt's thrill'd bosom leaps at Pleasure's
    smile;

Full oft, where Solitude and Silence dwell
Far far remote amid the lowly plain,

Resounds the voice of Woe from Virtue's cell.
Such is man's doom, and Pity weeps in vain.

Still grief recoils—How vainly have I strove
Thy power, O Melancholy, to withstand!
Tir'd I submit; but yet, O yet remove,
Or ease the pressure of thy heavy hand.

Yet for a while let the bewilder'd soul
Find in society relief from woe;
O yield a while to Friendship's soft controul;
Some respite, Friendship, wilt thou not bestow!

Come then, PHILANDER! for thy lofty mind
Looks down from far on all that charms the Great;
For thou canst bear, unshaken and resign'd,
The brightest smiles, the blackest frowns of Fate:

Come thou, whose love unlimited, sincere,
Nor faction cools, nor injury destroys;
Who lend'st to Misery's moans a pitying ear,
And feel'st with ecstacy another's joys:

Who know'st man's frailty; with a favouring eye,
And melting heart, behold'st a brother's fall;
Who unenslav'd by Custom's narrow tye
With manly freedom follow'st Reason's call.

And bring thy DELIA, softly-smiling Fair,
Whose spotless soul no sordid thoughts deform;
Her accents mild would still each throbbing care,
And harmonize the thunder of the storm:

Though blest with wisdom and with wit refin'd,
She courts not homage, nor desires to shine;

In Her each sentiment sublime is join'd
To female sweetness, and a form divine.

Come, and dispel the deep-surrounding shade:
Let chasten'd mirth the social hours employ;
O catch the swift-wing'd hour before 'tis fled,
On swiftest pinion flies the Hour of joy.

Even while the careless disencumber'd soul
Dissolving sinks to Joy's oblivious dream,
Even then to Time's tremendous verge we roll
With haste impetuous down life's surgy stream.

Can Gaiety the vanish'd years restore,
Or on the withering limbs fresh beauty shed,
Or soothe the sad INEVITABLE HOUR,
Or chear the dark dark mansions of the dead?

Still founds the solemn knell in Fancy's ear,
That call'd Cleora to the silent tomb;
To her how jocund roll'd the sprightly year!
How shone the nymph in Beauty's brightest bloom!

Ah! Beauty's bloom avails not in the grave,
Youth's lofty mien, nor Age's awful grace;
Moulder unknown the monarch and the slave
Whelm'd in th' enormous wreck of human race.

The thought-fix'd portraiture, the breathing bust,
The arch with proud memorials array'd,
The long-liv'd pyramid shall sink in dust
To dumb Oblivion's ever-desart shade.

Fancy from comfort wanders still astray.
Ah Melancholy! how I feel thy power!

Long have I labour'd to elude thy sway,
But 'tis enough, for I resist no more.

The traveler thus, that o'er the midnight-waste
Through many a lonesome path is doom'd to roam,
Wilder'd and weary sits him down at last;
For long the night, and distant far his home.

An ELEGY

Occasioned by the death of

A LADY.

SHALL unthinking man substantial deem
The forms that fleet through life's deceitful
    dream!
On clouds, where Fancy's beam amusive plays,
Shall heedless Hope his towering fabric raise!
Till at Death's touch the fairy visions fly,
And real scenes rush dismal on the eye,
And from elysium's soothing slumbers torn
The startled soul awakes, to think—and mourn.

O Ye, whose hours in jocund train advance,
To Joy's soft voice whose sprightly spirits dance,
Who flowery scenes in endless view survey
Glittering in beams of visionary day!
O yet while Fate delays th' impending woe
Be rous'd to thought, anticipate the blow;
Lest, like the lightning's glance, the sudden ill
Flash to confound, and penetrate to kill;
Lest thus involv'd in deep funereal gloom
With me ye bend o'er some untimely tomb,
Pour your wild ravings in Night's frighted ear,
And half pronounce Heaven's sacred doom severe.

 Wife! Beauteous! Good!—O every grace combin'd,
That charms the eye, that captivates the mind!
Fair—as the flower just opening to the view,
Whose leaves the Morning bathes in pearly dew!

F

Sweet—as the downy-pinion'd Gale, that roves
Fraught with the fragrance of Arabian groves!
Mild—as the strains, that, at the close of day
Warbling remote, along the vales decay!——
Yet, why with these compar'd? What tints so fine,
What sweetness, mildness, can be match'd with thine?
Why roam abroad? Since still to Fancy's eyes
I see I see the lov'd Idea rise.
Still let me gaze, and every care beguile,
Gaze on that cheek, where all the Graces smile;
That soul-expressing eye, whence, mildly bright
Fair Goodness beams on the transported sight;
That polish'd brow, where Wisdom sits serene,
Each feature forms, and dignifies the mien:
Still let me listen, while her words impart
Delight deep-thrilling through the glowing heart,

And all the soul, each tumult charm'd away,
Yields, gently led, to Virtue's easy sway.

Adorn'd by thee, bright Virtue, Age is young,
And music warbles from the faltering tongue;
Thy ray creative chears the clouded brow,
Flushes the faded cheek with rosy glow,
Illumes the joyless aspect, and supplies
A lively lustre to the languid eyes;
Each look, each accent, while it awes, invites;
And Age with every youthful grace delights:
But when Youth's bloom reflects thy brightening
    beams,
On the rapt view the blaze resistless streams,
Th' ecstatic breast triumphant Virtue warms,
And Beauty dazzles with angelic charms.*

Ah whither fled!—ye dear illusions stay!—
Lo, pale and silent lies the lovely clay!

---

* The Lady, whose death occasioned this Elegy, died at the age of twenty seven.

How are the roses on that lip decay'd
Which Health so late in vivid bloom array'd!
Health on her form each sprightly grace bestow'd,
With active life each speaking feature glow'd.
Fair was the flower, and soft the vernal sky;
Elate with hope we deem'd no tempest nigh;
When lo, a whirlwind's instantaneous gust
Laid all its beauties withering in the dust.
 All cold the hand, that sooth'd Woe's weary head!
All quench'd the eye, the pitying tear that shed!
All mute the voice, whose pleasing accents stole,
Infusing balm, into the rankled soul!—
O Death, why arm with cruelty thy power!
Why spare the weed, and lop the lovely flower!
Why fly thy shafts in lawless error driv'n!
Is Virtue then no more the care of heav'n!—

But, peace, bold thought! be still, my bursting
    heart!
We, not ELIZA, felt the fateful dart.
Scap'd the dark dungeon does the slave complain,
Nor bless the hand that broke the galling chain!
Say, pines not Virtue for the lingering morn,
On this dark desart doom'd to stray forlorn!
Where Reason's meteor-rays, with sickly glow,
O'er the dun gloom a dreadful glimmering throw,
Disclosing dubious to th' affrighted eye
O'erwhelming mountains tottering from on high,
Black billowy seas by endless tempests toss'd,
And weary ways in wildering labyrinths lost.
O happy stroke, that breaks the bonds of clay,
Darts through the bursting gloom the blaze of day,
And wings the soul with boundless flight to soar,
Where dangers threat, and fears alarm, no more.

Transporting thought! here let me wipe away
The falling tear, and wake a bolder lay.
But ah! afresh the swimming eye o'erflows——
Nor check the tear that streams for human woes—
Lo, o'er her dust, in speechless anguish, bend
The hopeless Parent, Husband, Brother, Friend!—
Vain hope of mortal man!—But cease thy strain,
Nor sorrow's dread solemnity profane;
Mix'd with yon drooping Mourners, o'er her bier
In silence shed the sympathetic tear.

THE HARES,

A FABLE.

LIFE is a jest. You call it worse,
   " A cheat, a snare, a clog, a curse.
" Tir'd of the long laborious strife
" You loathe the nauseous load of life.
" Through desarts dark perplex'd you stray,
" No beam to point the dreary way.
" In vain you call for aid. No friend
" Will deign a pitying look to lend.
" Hope comes at last, in courteous guise,
" With dimply cheek and smiling eyes;

" He points at some far-blazing toy,

" Incites your flight, assures the joy.

" Born on Hope's soaring wing you sweep

" Along the ether's azure deep.

" The phantom flies, but close behind

" Hope wafts you swifter than the wind.

" The meteor bursts; led far abroad

" You scarce regain your wonted road,

" Listless, fatigued. Before 'twas care,

" Now all is tumult and despair.

" Or if, long painful labour past,

" You catch the flying thing at last;

" Soon as you fondly grasp your prey,

" From your support Hope shrinks away.

" No more upborn on wings of Hope

" Prone through the empty air you drop:

" The glittering toy, that seem'd so late

" To gild the blackest clouds of fate,

"That lighten'd your severest toil,
"Each feature brightening with a smile,
"Now heavy, dark, and cumbrous all
"Serves but to aggravate your fall.
"Thus Hope, our smiling flattering friend,
"Proves our tormentor in the end;
"We're wretched if we miss our aim,
"And, that attain'd, we are the same.
"What slavish mortal then, you say,
"Would choose to drag this clog of clay,
"Nor longs to lay his weary head
"Secure on Death's dark dusty bed?"

 Yes, yes, I grant the sons of earth
Are doom'd to misery from their birth.
We all of sorrow have our share;
But say, Is yours beyond compare?
Look round the world: you'll quickly find
Each individual of our kind

Press'd with an equal load of ill;
Equal at least.   Look further still;
Let Reason's serious eye explore
What Passion slightly scan'd before.
In Poverty's sad sable cell
Attend to Famine's feeble wail:
Behold a meagre shivering form
Unfenc'd against the piercing storm.
Or view the couch where Sickness lies;
Mark his pale cheeks, his dizzy eyes,
His frame by strong convulsions torn,
His struggling sighs, and looks forlorn.
See, where transfix'd with fiercest pangs
O'er his heap'd hoard the miser hangs:
Whistles the wind—he starts, he stares,
Nor Slumber's balmy bounties shares;
Despair Remorse and Terror roll
Their tempests on his darken'd soul.

But now, perhaps, it may avail
T" enforce our reasoning with a tale.

Soft was the morn, the sky serene,
The jolly hunting band convene.
The huntsman sends around his eyes,
And oft in thought the game descries;
Now with bland words the steed addresses,
And now rhe frisking hound caresses:
The neighing steed impatient spurns,
Each beagle's breast with ardor burns.

That morn, a council of the hares
Was met on national affairs.
The chiefs were set; above their head
The furze its frizzled covering spread.
Long lists of grievances were heard;
By which in general it appear'd
That, one and all, the hares were bent
To plan anew the government.

Our harmless race shall every savage
Both quadruped and biped ravage?
The youth his father's only hopes,
Who gayly now the verdure crops,
Whose pulse beats strong in every vein,
Whose limbs leap light along the plain,
May yet ere noon (sad destiny!)
On some bare heath dismember'd lie.
Nor headlong Youth, nor cautious Age
Can scape the ruthless murderer's rage.
In every gale we hear the foe,
Each gale comes fraught with sounds of woe,
Each morning but awakes our fears,
Each evening sees us bath'd in tears.
But must we ever idly grieve,
Nor strive our fortunes to relieve?
Small is each individual's force,
Nor I from prudence boast resource:

But were our numerous tribes combin'd,
These murderers to their cost might find,
No foe is weak, whom Justice arms,
Whom Concord leads, and Hatred warms.
Who dares assert a righteous cause
From his own heart obtains applause.
Be rous'd; or liberty acquire,
Or in the great attempt expire.

   Here labouring in his heaving breast
The swelling thought his voice suppress'd;
Despair, Revenge, their rage supply,
And flash from each indignant eye.

   Meanwhile the clamours of the war
Mingling confus'dly from afar
Swell in the wind. Now louder cries
Distinct of men and hounds arise.
Forth from the brake, with beating heart,
Th' assembled hares tumultuous start,

And, every straining nerve on wing,
Away precipitately spring.
The hunting band, a signal given,
Thick-thundring o'er the plain are driven;
O'er cliff abrupt, and shrubby mound,
And river broad impetuous bound,
Now plunge amid the forest shades,
Glance through the openings of the glades,
Now o'er the level lawn they sweep,
Now with short steps strain up the steep;
While backward from the hunter's eyes
The landscape like a torrent flies.
At last an antient wood they gain'd
By pruner's ax yet unprofan'd.
High o'er the rest, by Nature rear'd
The oak's majestic boughs appear'd.
Below, a copse of various hue
In barbarous luxuriance grew;

No knife had curb'd the rambling sprays,
No hand had wove th' implicit maze.
The flowering thorn self-taught to wind
The hazle's stubborn stem entwin'd,
The prickly bramble flaunted round,
And rough furze crept along the ground.
Here shelter'd from the storms of fate
The hares enjoy a safe retreat.
The hunting band in vain essay
Through the thick shrubs to force their way;
Th' impatient beagle yelps in vain,
In vain the courser spurns the plain,
In vain the huntsman vents his ire
In threats and execrations dire.
Thus from the field of death reliev'd
When Troy her trembling sons receiv'd,
Achilles curs'd invidious fate,
And thunder'd at the Scæan gate.

The western wind now waxing loud
Tumultuous roar'd along the wood;
From rustling leaves and crashing boughs
The sound of woe and war arose.

The hares distracted scour the grove,
As terror and amazement drove,
But danger, wheresoe'er they fled,
Still seem'd impending o'er their head.

Now throng'd amidst a grotto's gloom,
All hopes extinct, they wait their doom.
Dire was the silence, till, at length,
Even from despair deriving strength
A daring youth these words address'd,
Which oft the bursting throb suppress'd.

O race! the scorn, the sport of fate,
With every sort of ill beset,
And curst with keenest sense to feel
The sharpest sting of every ill!

We sure by Nature were design'd
Most wretched of the wretched kind.
Say ye, who, fraught with mighty scheme,
Of liberty and vengeance dream,
What now remains? In what recess
Hope we to taste the sweets of peace,
Since Fate on every side prepares
For us inextricable snares?
Are we alone of all beneath
Condemn'd to misery worse than death?
Must we with fruitless labour strive
In misery worse than death to live?
No. Be the lesser ill our choice,
So dictates Nature's prompting voice;
'Tis Nature bids us dare to die,
And disappoint our destiny.
Who grudges momentary pain,
A short relief from woe to gain?

Death's pangs but for a moment laſt;
And when that tranſient ill is paſt,
Our ſorrows are for ever fled,
For not even dreams moleſt the dead.
Thus while he ſpoke, his words impart
The dire reſolve to every heart.

 A diſtant lake in proſpect lay,
That glittering in the ſolar ray
Gleam'd through the duſky trees, and ſpread
A languid radiance o'er the ſhade.
Thither with one conſent they bend,
Their miſeries with their lives to end.
Through the thick wood proceed the train,
And now they reach the open plain,
And onward with redoubled force
Stung with deſpair impel their courſe;
While each in thought already hears
The waters hiſſing in his ears.

Fast by the margin of the lake,
Conceal'd within a thorny brake
A linnet sate, whose careless lay
Amus'd the solitary day.

Careless he sung, for on his breast
Sorrow no lasting trace imprest.
When suddenly he hears the sound
Of swift feet trampling thick the ground.
Light to a neighbouring tree he flies;
Thence trembling sends around his eyes;
No foe appear'd; his fears were vain;
Pleas'd he renews the sprightly strain.

The hares, whose noise had caus'd his fright,
Saw with surprise the linnet's flight.
Is there on earth a wretch, they said,
Whom our approach can strike with dread?
An instantaneous flow of thought
To tumult every bosom wrought;

Amaz'd they stood, nor words could find
T' express the working of their mind.
So fares the system-builder sage,
Who, plodding on from youth to age,
At last on some foundation-dream
Has rear'd aloft his goodly scheme;
Has prov'd his predecessors fools,
And bound all nature by his rules;
So fares he in that dreadful hour,
When Truth exerts her sacred power,
Some new phænomenon to raise,
Which, bursting on his frighted gaze,
From its high summit to the ground
Proves the whole edifice unsound.

 An antient hare, whose mind sedate
Had often prov'd th' extremes of fate,
Compos'd at length in voice and look,
The thought-bewilder'd band bespoke.

Children, says he, th' attentive mind
In slight events will often find
Of sound instruction fresh supplies,
Which Reason's scanty store denies.
That our afflictions were the worst,
And we, beyond all others, curst
With woes remediless, of late
Seem'd certain as the laws of fate:
When lo, an accident so slight
As yonder little linnet's flight
Has made your stubborn hearts confess,
(So your amazement bids me guess)
That all your load of woes and fears
Is but a part of what he bears.
Where can he rest secure from harms,
Whom even a helpless hare alarms?
Yet he repines not at his lot;
When past his dangers are forgot:

On yonder bough he trims his wings,
And with unufual rapture fings.
While we, lefs wretched, fink beneath
Our lighter ills, and rufh to death!——
No more of this unmeaning rage,
But hear, my friends, the words of Age:
From glozing Art no aid I feek,
In me you hear Experience fpeak.

   When by the winds of Autumn driven
The fcatter'd clouds fly 'crofs the heaven,
Oft have we from fome mountain's head
Beheld th' alternate light and fhade
Sweep o'er the vale: here hovering low'rs
The fhadowy cloud; there downward pours
Streaming direct a flood of day,
That from the view flies fwift away:
It flies, while other fhades advance,
And other ftreaks of funfhine glance.

Thus chequer'd is life's various maze
With misery's clouds, and pleasure's rays.
Then hope not, while you journey on,
Still to be basking in the sun;
Nor dread, though now in shades you mourn,
That sunshine will no more return.
If by betraying fear o'ercome
You fly before th' approaching gloom,
And strive to leave your woe behind;
The labour vain you soon will find;
The cloud pursues with equal speed,
And still hangs frowning o'er your head.
Who longs to reach the radiant plain
Must onward urge his course amain;
For doubly swift the shadow flies,
When 'gainst the gale the pilgrim plies.
Or though unequal to support
The labour of that great effort,

Which struggles through involving woe;
Yet ne'er your fortitude forego;
Shrink not; but firm and undismay'd
Maintain your ground; the fleeting shade
Ere long spontaneous glides away,
And gives you back th' enlivening ray.
Lo, while I speak, our danger's past:
No more the shrill horn's angry blast
Rings in our ears; the savage roar
Of war and murder now is o'er.
Then snatch the joy which fate allows,
Careless of past or future woes.

 He spoke: each breast is sooth'd to peace,
Complacence softens every face,
And hope revives; the hateful lake
That instant one and all forsake,
In sweet amusement to employ
The present sprightly hour of joy.

Now from the western mountain's brow,
Compact with clouds of various glow
The sun a broader orb displays,
And shoots aslope his ruddy rays.
The lawn assumes a yellower green,
And dew-drops spangle all the scene.
The fragrant gale sighs soft along,
The shepherd chaunts his simple song,
With all their lays the groves resound,
And falling waters murmur round;
Discord and Care were put to flight,
And all was peace and calm delight.

EPITAPH

ON ✶✶✶✶✶ ✶✶✶✶✶✶

ESCAP'D the gloom of mortal life, a foul
   Here leaves its mouldering tenement of clay,
Safe, where no Cares their whelming billows roll,
No Doubts bewilder, and no Hopes betray.

   Like thee, I once have stemm'd the sea of life;
Like thee, have languish'd after empty joys;
Like thee, have labour'd in the stormy strife;
Been griev'd for trifles, and amus'd with toys.

Yet for a while 'gainst Passion's threatful blast
Let steady Reason urge the struggling oar;
Shot through the dreary gloom the morn at last
Gives to thy longing eye the blisful shore.

Forget my frailties, thou art also frail;
Forgive my lapses, for thyself mayst fall;
Nor read unmov'd my artless tender tale,
I was a friend, O man, to thee, to all.

EPITAPH.

TO this grave is committed
All that the Grave can claim
Of two Brothers ***** and **** ******
Who on the VII of October MDCCLVII,
Both unfortunately perished in the * * * water:
The one in his XXII, the other in his XVIII year.
Their disconsolate Father **************
Erects this monument to the memory of
These amiable Youths;
Whose early virtues promised
Uncommon comfort to his declining years,
And singular emolument to society.

O Thou! whose steps in sacred reverence tread
These lone dominions of the silent Dead;

On this sad stone a pious look bestow,
Nor uninstructed read this tale of woe;
And while the sigh of sorrow heaves thy breast,
Let each rebellious murmur be suppress'd;
Heaven's hidden ways to trace, for us, how vain!
Heaven's wise decrees, how impious, to arraign!
Pure from the stains of a polluted age,
In early bloom of life, THEY left the stage:
Not doom'd in lingering woe to waste their breath
One moment snatch'd Them from the power of Death:
They liv'd united, and united died;
Happy the friends, whom Death cannot divide!

NOVEMBER 1st. 1757.

    This Epitaph is engraven on a tombstone in the church-yard of *Lethnet* in the shire of *Angus*.

ELEGY.

TIR'D with the busy crouds, that all the day
    Impatient throng where Folly's altars flame,
My languid powers dissolve with quick decay,
Till genial Sleep repair the sinking frame.

Hail kind Reviver! that canst lull the cares,
    And every weary sense compose to rest,
Lighten th' oppressive load which Anguish bears,
    And warm with hope the cold desponding breast.

Touch'd by thy rod, from Power's majestic brow
    Drops the gay plume; he pines a lowly clown;
And on the cold earth stretch'd the son of Woe
    Quaffs Pleasure's draught, and wears a fancy'd crown.

When rous'd by thee, on boundless pinions born
Fancy to fairy scenes exults to rove,
Now scales the cliff gay-gleaming on the morn,
Now sad and silent treads the deepening grove;

Or skims the main, and listens to the storms,
Marks the long waves roll far remote away;
Or mingling with ten thousand glittering forms
Floats on the gale, and basks in purest day.

Haply, ere long, pierc'd by the howling blast
Through dark and pathless desarts I shall roam,
Plunge down th' unfathom'd deep, or shrink aghast
Where bursts the shrieking spectre from the tomb:

Perhaps loose Luxury's enchanting smile
Shall lure my steps to some romantic dale,

Where Mirth's light freaks th' unheeded hours
       beguile,
And airs of rapture warble in the gale.

Inſtructive emblem of this mortal ſtate!
Where ſcenes as various every hour ariſe
In ſwift ſucceſſion, which the hand of Fate
Preſents, then ſnatches from our wondering eyes.

Be taught, vain man, how fleeting all thy joys,
Thy boaſted grandeur, and thy glittering ſtore;
Death comes, and all thy fancy'd bliſs deſtroys,
Quick as a dream it fades, and is no more.

And, ſons of Sorrow! though the threatening
       ſtorm
Of angry Fortune overhang a while,
Let not her frowns your inward peace deform;
Soon happier days in happier climes ſhall ſmile.

Through earth's throng'd visions while we toss
  forlorn,
'Tis tumult all, and rage, and restless strife;
But these shall vanish like the dreams of morn,
When Death awakes us to immortal life.

SONG

In Imitation of SHAKESPEAR's

Blow, blow, thou winter wind &c.

BLOW, blow, thou vernal gale!
Thy balm will not avail
To ease my aching breast;
Though thou the billows smoothe,
Thy murmurs cannot soothe
My weary soul to rest.

Flow, flow, thou tuneful stream!
Infuse the easy dream
Into the peaceful soul;

But thou canst not compose
The tumult of my woes,
Though soft thy waters roll.

Blush, blush, ye fairest flowers!
Beauties surpassing yours
My Rosalind adorn;
Nor is the winter's blast,
That lays your glories waste,
So killing as her scorn.

Breathe, breathe, ye tender lays,
That linger down the maze
Of yonder winding grove;
O let your soft controul
Bend her relenting soul
To pity and to love.

Fade, fade, ye flowrets fair!
Gales, fan no more the air!
Ye streams forget to glide!
Be hush'd, each vernal strain!
Since nought can soothe my pain,
Nor mitigate her pride.

ANACREON, Ode 22.

Παρὰ τὴν σκίην, βάθυλλε,
Κάθισον————

BATHYLLUS, in yonder lone grove
All carelesly let us recline:
To shade us the branches above
Their leaf-waving tendrils combine;
While a streamlet inviting repose
Soft-murmuring wanders away,
And gales warble wild through the boughs:
Who there would not pass the sweet day?

THE

THE BEGINNING OF THE FIRST BOOK OF

LUCRETIUS

TRANSLATED.

Æneadum Genetrix————v. 1——45.

MOTHER of mighty Rome's imperial line,
    Delight of man, and of the Powers divine,
VENUS, all-bounteous queen! whose genial pow'r
Diffuses beauty in unbounded store
Through seas, and fertile plains, and all that lies
Beneath the starr'd expansion of the skies.
Prepar'd by thee, the embryo springs to day,
And opes its eyelids on the golden ray.

At thy approach, the clouds tumultuous fly,
And the hush'd storms in gentle breezes die;
Flowers instantaneous spring; the billows sleep;
A wavy radiance smiles along the deep;
At thy approach, th' untroubled sky refines,
And all serene heaven's lofty concave shines.
Soon as her blooming form the Spring reveals,
And Zephyr breathes his warm prolific gales,
The feather'd tribes first catch the genial flame,
And to the groves thy glad return proclaim.
Thence to the beasts the soft infection spreads;
The raging cattle spurn the grassy meads,
Burst o'er the plains, and frantic in their course
Cleave the wild torrents with resistless force.
Won by thy charms thy dictates all obey,
And eager follow where thou lead'st the way.
Whatever haunts the mountains, or the main,
The rapid river, or the verdant plain,

Or forms its leafy manfion in the fhades,
All, all thy univerfal power pervades,
Each panting bofom melts to foft defires,
And with the love of propagation fires.
And fince thy fovereign influence guides the reins
Of Nature, and the Univerfe fuftains;
Since nought without thee burfts the bonds of
        Night,
To hail the happy realms of heavenly light;
Since love, and joy, and harmony are thine;
Guide me, O Goddefs, by thy power divine,
And to my rifing lays thy fuccour bring,
While I the UNIVERSE attempt to fing.
O, may my verfe deferv'd applaufe obtain
Of Him, for whom I try the daring ftrain,
My MEMMIUS, Him, whom thou profufely kind
Adorn'ft with every excellence refin'd.
And that immortal charms my fong may grace,
Let war, with all its cruel labours, ceafe;

O hush the dismal din of arms once more,
And calm the jarring world from shore to shore.
By thee alone the race of man foregoes
The rage of blood, and sinks in soft repose:
For mighty Mars the dreadful God of arms,
Who wakes or stills the battle's dire alarms,
In love's strong fetters by thy charms is bound,
And languishes with an eternal wound.
Oft from his bloody toil the God retires
To quench in thy embrace his fierce desires.
Soft on thy heaving bosom he reclines,
And round thy yielding neck transported twines;
There fix'd in ecstacy intense surveys
Thy kindling beauties with insatiate gaze,
Grows to thy balmy mouth, and ardent sips
Celestial sweets from thy ambrosial lips.
O, while the God with fiercest raptures blest
Lies all dissolving on thy sacred breast,

O breathe thy melting whispers to his ear,
And bid him still the loud alarms of war.
In these tumultuous days, the Muse, in vain,
Her steady tenor lost, pursues the strain,
And MEMMIUS' generous soul disdains to taste
The calm delights of philosophic rest;
Paternal fires his beating breast inflame,
To rescue Rome, and vindicate her name.

L. HORACE,

HORACE,

BOOK II. Ode 10.

TRANSLATED.

Rectius vives, Licini————

WOULDST thou through life securely glide;
Nor boundless o'er the ocean ride;
Nor ply too near th' insidious shore,
Scar'd at the tempest's threatning roar.

The man, who follows Wisdom's voice,
And makes the GOLDEN MEAN his choice,
Nor plung'd in antique gloomy cells
Midst hoary desolation dwells;
Nor to allure the envious eye
Rears his proud palace to the sky.

The pine, that all the grove transcends,
With every blast the tempest rends;

Totters the tower with thundrous sound,
And spreads a mighty ruin round;
Jove's bolt with desolating blow
Strikes the etherial mountain's brow.

The man, whose stedfast soul can bear
Fortune indulgent or severe,
Hopes when she frowns, and when she smiles
With cautious fear eludes her wiles.
Jove with rude winter wastes the plain,
Jove decks the rosy spring again.
Life's former ills are overpast,
Nor will the present always last.
Now Phœbus wings his shafts, and now
He lays aside th' unbended bow,
Strikes into life the trembling string,
And wakes the silent muse to sing.

With unabating courage, brave
Adversity's tumultuous wave;

When too propitious breezes rise,
And the light vessel swiftly flies,
With timid caution catch the gale,
And shorten the distended sail.

HORACE,

BOOK III. Ode 13.

TRANSLATED.

O Fons Blandusiæ———

BLANDUSIA! more than chrystal clear!
   Whose soothing murmurs charm the ear!
Whose margin soft with flowrets crown'd
Invites the festive band around,

Their careless limbs diffus'd supine,
To quaff the soul-enlivening wine.

To thee a tender kid I vow,
That aims for fight his budding brow;
In thought, the wrathful combat proves,
Or wantons with his little loves:
But vain are all his purpos'd schemes,
Delusive all his flattering dreams,
To morrow shall his fervent blood
Stain the pure silver of thy flood.

When fiery Sirius blasts the plain,
Untouch'd thy gelid streams remain.
To thee, the fainting flocks repair,
To taste thy cool reviving air;
To thee, the ox with toil opprest,
And lays his languid limbs to rest.

As springs of old renown'd, thy name
Blest fountain! I devote to fame;

Thus while I sing in deathless lays
The verdant holm, whose waving sprays,
Thy sweet retirement to defend,
High o'er the moss-grown rock impend,
Whence prattling in loquacious play
Thy sprightly waters leap away.

THE

PASTORALS

OF

VIRGIL

TRANSLATED.

Non ita certandi cupidus, quam propter a-
morem
Quod *TE IMITARI* aveo———
       Lucret. Lib. III.

THE PASTORALS OF

VIRGIL.

THE FIRST PASTORAL.

MELIBOEUS, TITYRUS.

MELIBOEUS.

WHERE the broad beeche an ample shade displays,
Your slender reed resounds the sylvan lays,
O happy TITYRUS! while we, forlorn,
Driven from our lands, to distant climes are born,

It has been observed by some critics, who have treated of Pastoral Poetry, that, in every Poem of this kind, it is proper, that the scene

Stretch'd careless in the peaceful shade you sing,

And all the groves with AMARYLLIS ring.

TITYRUS.

THIS peace to a propitious God I owe;

None else, my friend, such blessings could bestow.

Him will I celebrate with rites divine,

And frequent lambs shall stain his sacred shrine.

or landscape, connected with the little plot or fable on which the poem is founded, be delineated with at least as much accuracy, as is sufficient to render the description particular and picturesque. How far Virgil has thought fit to attend to such a rule may appear from the remarks which the Translator has subjoined to every Pastoral.

 The scene of the first Pastoral is pictured out with great accuracy. The shepherds Meliboeus and Tityrus are represented as conversing together beneath a spreading beeche-tree. Flocks and herds are feeding hard by. At a little distance we behold, on the one hand a great rock, and on the other a fence of flowering willows. The prospect as it widens is diversified with groves, and streams, and some tall trees particularly elms. Beyond all these appear marshy grounds, and rocky hills. The ragged and drooping flock of the unfortunate shepherd, particularly the she-goat which he leads along, are no inconsiderable figures in this picture.—The time is the evening of a summer-day, a little before sunset. See of the Original v. 1, 5, 9, 52, 54, 57, 59, 81, &c.

 This Pastoral is said to have been written on the following occasion. Augustus, in order to reward the services of his Veterans, by means of whom he had established himself in the Roman empire, distributed among them the lands that lay contiguous to Mantua and Cremona.

By Him, these feeding herds in safety stray;
By Him, in peace I pipe the rural lay.

MELIBOEUS.

I ENVY not, but wonder at your fate,
That no alarms invade this blest retreat;
While neighbouring fields the voice of woe re-
    sound,
And desolation rages all around.
Worn with fatigue I slowly onward bend,
And scarce my feeble fainting goats attend.
My hand this sickly dam can hardly bear,
Whose young new-yean'd (ah once an hopeful
    pair!)
Amid the tangling hazles as they lay,
On the sharp flint were left to pine away.

Cremona. To make way for these intruders, the rightful Owners, of whom Virgil was one, were turned out. But our Poet, by the intercession of Mecænas, was reinstated in his possessions. Meliboeus here personates one of the unhappy exiles, and Virgil is represented under the character of Tityrus.

These ills I had foreseen, but that my mind
To all portents and prodigies was blind.
Oft have the blasted oaks foretold my woe;
And often has the inauspicious crow,
Perch'd on the wither'd holm, with fateful cries
Scream'd in my ear her dismal prophecies.
But say, O TITYRUS, What God bestows
This blisful life of undisturb'd repose?

TITYRUS.

IMPERIAL Rome, while yet to me unknown,
I vainly liken'd to our country-town,
Our little Mantua, at which is sold
The yearly offspring of our fruitful fold:
As in the whelp the father's shape appears,
And as the kid its mother's semblance bears.
Thus greater things my inexperienc'd mind
Rated by others of inferior kind.
But SHE, midst other cities, rears her head
High, as the cypress overtops the reed.

MELIBOEUS.

And why to visit Rome was you inclin'd?

TITYRUS.

'Twas there I hoped my liberty to find.
And there my liberty I found at last,
Though long with listless indolence opprest;
Yet not till Time had silver'd o'er my hairs,
And I had told a tedious length of years;
* Nor till the gentle AMARYLLIS charm'd,
And GALATEA's love no longer warm'd.
For (to my friend I will confess the whole)
While GALATEA captive held my soul,
Languid and lifeless all I drag'd the chain,
Neglected liberty, neglected gain.
Though from my fold the frequent victim bled,
Though my fat cheese th' ungrateful city fed,

---

* Nor till the gentle Amaryllis —] The refinements of Taubmannus, De La Cerda, and others, who will have Amaryllis to signify Rome, and Galatea to signify Mantua, have perplexed this passage not a little: if the literal meaning be admitted, the whole becomes obvious and natural.

For this I ne'er perceiv'd my wealth increase;
I lavish'd all her haughty heart to please.

MELIBOEUS.

WHY AMARYLLIS pin'd, and pass'd away
In lonely shades the melancholy day;
Why to the Gods she breath'd incessant vows;
For whom her mellow apples press'd the boughs
So late, I wonder'd-----TITYRUS was gone,
And she (ah luckless maid!) was left alone.
Your absence every warbling fountain mourn'd,
And woods and wilds the wailing strains return'd.

TITYRUS.

WHAT could I do? To break th' enslaving chain
All other efforts had (alas!) been vain;
Nor durst my hopes presume, but there, to find
The Gods so condescending and so kind.

'Twas there these eyes the heaven-born YOUTH*
  beheld,
To whom our altars monthly incense yield:
My suit He even prevented, while He spoke,
" Manure your antient farm, and feed your former
  flock."

MELIBOEUS.

HAPPY old man! then shall your lands remain,
Extent sufficient for th' industrious swain!
Though bleak and bare yon ridgy rocks arise,
And lost in lakes the neighbouring pasture lies.
Your herds on wonted grounds shall safely range,
And never feel the dire effects of change.
No foreign flock shall spread infecting bane
To hurt your pregnant dams, thrice happy swain!
You by known streams and sacred fountains laid
Shall taste the coolness of the fragrant shade.

---

* Augustus Cæsar.

Beneath yon fence, where willow-boughs unite,
And to their flowers the swarming bees invite,
Oft shall the lulling hum persuade to rest,
And balmy slumbers steal into your breast;
While warbled from this rock the Pruner's lay
In deep repose dissolves your soul away;
High on yon elm the turtle wails alone,
And your lov'd ringdoves breathe a hoarser moan.

TITYRUS.

The nimble harts shall graze in empty air,
And seas retreating leave their fishes bare,
The German dwell where rapid Tigris flows,
The Parthian banish'd by invading foes
Shall drink the Gallic Arar, from my breast
Ere His majestic image be effac'd.

MELIBOEUS.

But we must travel o'er a length of lands,
O'er Scythian snows, or Afric's burning sands;

Some wander where remote Oäxes laves
The Cretan meadows with his rapid waves;
In Britain some, from every comfort torn,
From all the world remov'd, are doom'd to mourn.
When long long years have tedious roll'd away,
Ah! shall I yet at last, at last, survey
My dear paternal lands, and dear abode,
Where once I reign'd in walls of humble sod!
These lands, these harvests must the soldier share!
For rude barbarians lavish we our care!
How are our fields become the spoil of wars!
How are we ruin'd by intestine jars!
Now, MELIBOEUS, now ingraff the pear,
Now teach the vine its tender sprays to rear!----
Go then, my goats!---go, once an happy store!
Once happy!----happy now (alas!) no more!
No more shall I, beneath the bowery shade
In rural quiet indolently laid,

Behold you from afar the cliffs afcend,

And from the fhrubby precipice depend;

No more to mufic wake my melting flute,

While on the thyme you feed, and willow's whole-
fome fhoot.

TITYRUS.

This night at leaft with me you may repofe

On the green foliage, and forget your woes.

Apples and nuts mature our boughs afford,

And curdled milk in plenty crowns my board.

Now from yon hamlets clouds of fmoke arife,

And flowly roll along the evening-fkies;

And fee projected from the mountain's brow

A lengthen'd fhade obfcures the plain below.

THE SECOND PASTORAL.

ALEXIS.

YOUNG CORYDON for fair ALEXIS pin'd,
 But hope ne'er gladden'd his desponding mind;
Nor vows nor tears the scornful boy could move,
Distinguish'd by his wealthier master's love.

The chief excellency of this Poem consists in its delicacy and simplicity. Corydon addresses his favourite in such a purity of sentiment as one would think might effectually discountenance the prepossessions which generally prevail against the subject of this eclogue. The nature of his affection may easily be ascertained from his ideas of the happiness which he hopes to enjoy in the company of his beloved Alexis.

 O tantum libeat——
 O deign at last amid these lonely fields &c.

It appears to have been no other than that friendship, which was encouraged by the wisest legislators of antient Greece, as a noble incentive

Oft to the beeche's deep-embowering shade
Pensive and sad this hapless shepherd stray'd;
There told in artless verse his tender pain
To echoing hills and groves, but all in vain.

In vain the flute's complaining lays I try;
And am I doom'd, unpitying boy, to die?
Now to faint flocks the grove a shade supplies,
And in the thorny brake the lizard lies;
Now THESTYLIS with herbs of savoury taste
Prepares the weary harvestman's repast;
And all is still, save where the buzzing found
Of chirping grashoppers is heard around;
While I expos'd to all the rage of heat
Wander the wilds in search of thy retreat.

centive to virtue, and recommended by the example even of Agesilaus, Pericles and Socrates: an affection wholly distinct from the infamous attachments that prevailed among the licentious. The Reader will find a full and satisfying account of this generous passion in Dr. Potter's antiquities of Greece B. iv. Chap. 9 Monf. Bayle in his Dictionary at the article *Virgile* has at great length vindicated our Poet from the charge of immorality which the Critics have grounded upon this pastoral.

The

Was it not eaſier to ſupport the pain
I felt from AMARYLLIS' fierce diſdain?
Eaſier MENALCAS' cold neglect to bear,
Black though he was, though thou art blooming
    fair?
Yet be relenting, nor too much preſume,
O beauteous boy, on thy celeſtial bloom;
The ſable * violet yields a precious die,
While uſeleſs on the field the withering lillies lie.
Ah cruel boy! my love is all in vain,
No thoughts of thine regard thy wretched ſwain.
How rich my flock thou careſt not to know,
Nor how my pails with generous milk o'erflow.
With bleat of thouſand lambs my hills reſound,
And all the year my milky ſtores abound.

  The ſcene of this Paſtoral is a grove interſperſed with beeche trees; the ſeaſon, harveſt.

  * The ſable violet) Vaccinium (here tranſlated *violet*) yielded a purple colour uſed in dying the garments of ſlaves, according to Plin. l. xvi, c. 28.

Not AMPHION's lays were sweeter than my song,
Those lays that led the listening herds along.
And if the face be true I lately view'd,
Where calm and clear th' uncurling ocean stood,
I lack not beauty, nor couldst thou deny,
That even with DAPHNIS I may dare to vie.
 O deign at last amid these lonely fields,
To taste the pleasures which the country yields;
With me to dwell in cottages resign'd,
To roam the woods, to shoot the bounding hind;
With me the weanling kids from home to guide
To the green mallows on the mountain-side;
With me in echoing groves the song to raise,
And emulate even PAN's celestial lays.
PAN taught the jointed reed its tuneful strain,
PAN guards the tender flock, and shepherd swain.
Nor grudge, ALEXIS, that the rural pipe
So oft hath stain'd the roses of thy lip:

How did AMYNTAS strive thy skill to gain!
How grieve at last to find his labour vain!
Of seven unequal reeds a pipe I have,
The precious gift which good DAMOETAS gave;
Take this, the dying shepherd said, for none
Inherits all my skill but thou alone.
He said; AMYNTAS murmurs at my praise,
And with an envious eye the gift surveys.
Besides, as presents for my soul's delight
Two beauteous kids I keep bestreak'd with white,
Nourish'd with care, nor purchas'd without pain;
An ewe's full udder twice a day they drain.
These to obtain oft THESTYLIS hath tried
Each winning art, while I her suit deny'd;
But I at last shall yield what she requests,
Since thy relentless pride my gifts detests.

Come, beauteous boy, and bless my rural bowers.
For thee the nymphs collect the choicest flowers:

Fair NAIS culls amid the bloomy dale
The drooping poppy, and the violet pale,
To marygolds the hyacinth applies,
Shading the glossy with the tawny dies:
Narcissus' flower with daffodil entwin'd,
And casia's breathing sweets to these are join'd,
With every bloom that paints the vernal grove,
And all to form a garland for my Love.
Myself with sweetest fruits will crown thy feast;
The luscious peach shall gratify thy taste,
And chesnut brown (once high in my regard,
For AMARYLLIS this to all prefer'd;
But if the blushing plum thy choice thou make,
The plum shall more be valued for thy sake.)
The myrtle wreath'd with laurel shall exhale
A blended fragrance to delight thy smell.

Ah CORYDON! thou rustic, simple swain!
Thyself, thy prayers, thy offers all are vain.

How few, compar'd with rich IOLAS store,
Thy boasted gifts, and all thy wealth how poor!
Wretch that I am! while thus I pine forlorn,
And all the live-long day inactive mourn,
The boars have laid my silver fountains waste,
My flowers are fading in the southern blast.----
Fly'st thou, ah foolish boy, the lonesome grove?
Yet Gods for this have left the realms above.
PARIS with scorn the pomp of Troy survey'd,
And sought th' Idæan bowers and peaceful shade.
In her proud palaces let PALLAS shine;
The lowly woods, and rural life be mine.
The lioness all dreadful in her course
Pursues the wolf, and he with headlong force
Flies at the wanton goat, that loves to climb
The cliff's steep side, and crop the flowering thyme;
Thee CORYDON pursues, O beauteous boy:
Thus each is drawn along by some peculiar joy.

Now evening soft comes on; and homeward now
From field the weary oxen bear the plough.
The setting sun now beams more mildly bright,
The shadows lengthening with the level light.
While with love's flame my restless bosom glows,
For love no interval of ease allows.
Ah CORYDON! to weak complaints a prey!
What madness thus to waste the fleeting day!
Be rous'd at length; thy half-prun'd vines demand
The needful culture of thy curbing hand.
Haste, lingering swain, the flexile willows weave,
And with thy wonted care thy wants relieve.
Forget ALEXIS' unrelenting scorn,
Another Love thy passion will return.

THE THIRD PASTORAL.

MENALCAS, DAMOETAS, PALÆMON.

MENALCAS.

TO whom belongs this flock, DAMOETAS, pray:
To MELIBOEUS?

DAMOETAS.

No; the other day
The shepherd ÆGON gave it me to keep.

The contending shepherds Menalcas and Damœtas, together with their umpire Palæmon, are seated on the grass, not far from a row of beeche-trees. Flocks are seen feeding hard by. The time of the day seems to be noon, the season between spring and summer,

MENALCAS.

† Ah still neglected, still unhappy sheep!
He plies NEÆRA with assiduous love,
And fears lest she my happier flame approve;
Meanwhile this hireling wretch (disgrace to swains!)
Defrauds his master, and purloins his gains,
Milks twice an hour, and drains the famish'd dams,
Whose empty dugs in vain attract the lambs.

DAMOETAS.

Forbear on men such language to bestow.
Thee, stain of manhood! thee, full well I know.
* I know, with whom---and where---(their grove defil'd
The nymphs reveng'd not, but indulgent smil'd)

† Throughout the whole of this altercation, notwithstanding the untoward subject, the Reader will find in the Original such a happy union of simplicity and force of expression and harmony of verse, as it is vain to look for in an English translation.

* The abruptness and obscurity of the Original is here imitated.

And how the goats beheld, then browzing near,
The shameful sight with a lascivious leer.

MENALCAS.

No doubt, when M<small>YCON</small>'s tender trees I broke,
And gash'd his young vines with a blunted hook.

DAMOETAS.

O<small>R</small> when conceal'd behind this antient row
Of beeche, you broke young D<small>APHNIS</small>' shafts and bow,
With sharpest pangs of rancorous anguish stung
To see the gift confer'd on one so young;
And had you not thus wreak'd your sordid spite,
Of very envy you had died outright.

MENALCAS.

G<small>ODS</small>! what may masters dare, when such a pitch
Of impudence their thievish hirelings reach!

Did I not, wretch (deny it if you dare)
Did I not see you DAMON's goat ensnare?
Lycisca bark'd; then I the felon spy'd,
And "Whither slinks yon sneaking thief"? I cry'd.
The thief discover'd straight his prey forsook,
And skulk'd amid the sedges of the brook.

DAMOETAS.

THAT goat my pipe from DAMON fairly
 gain'd;
A match was set, and I the prize obtain'd.
He own'd it due to my superior skill,
And yet refus'd his bargain to fulfil.

MENALCAS.

BY your superior skill-----the goat was won!
Have you a jointed pipe, indecent clown!
Whose whizzing straws with harshest discord jar'd,
As in the streets your wretched rhymes you mar'd.

DAMOETAS.

Boasts are but vain. I'm ready, when you will,
To make a solemn trial of our skill.
I stake this heifer, no ignoble prize;
Two calves from her full udder she supplies,
And twice a day her milk the pail o'erflows;
What pledge of equal worth will you expose?

MENALCAS.

Ought from the flock I dare not risque; I fear
A cruel stepdame, and a sire severe,
Who of their store so strict a reckoning keep,
That twice a-day they count the kids and sheep.
But, since you purpose to be mad to-day,
Two beechen cups I scruple not to lay,
(Whose far superior worth yourself will own)
The labour'd work of fam'd ALCIMEDON.

Rais'd round the brims by the engraver's care
The flaunting vine unfolds its foliage fair;
Entwin'd the ivy's tendrils seem to grow,
Half-hid in leaves its mimic berries glow:
Two figures rise below, of curious frame,
CONON, and---what's that other sage's name,
Who with his rod describ'd the world's vast round,
Taught when to reap, and when to till the ground.
At home I have reserv'd them unprofan'd,
No lip has e'er their glossy polish stain'd.

DAMOETAS.

Two cups for me that skilful Artist made;
Their handles with acanthus are array'd;
ORPHEUS is in the midst, whose magic song
Leads in tumultuous dance the lofty groves a-
  long.
At home I have reserv'd them unprofan'd,
No lip has e'er their glossy polish stain'd.

But my pledg'd heifer if aright you prize,
The cups so much extol'd you will despise.

MENALCAS.

These arts, proud boaster, all are lost on me;
To any terms I readily agree.
You shall not boast your victory to-day,
Let him be judge who passes first this way;
And see the good PALÆMON! trust me, swain,
You'll be more cautious how you brag again.

DAMOETAS.

Delays I brook not; if you dare, proceed;
At singing no antagonist I dread.
PALÆMON listen to th' important songs,
To such debates attention strict belongs.

PALÆMON.

Sing then. A couch the flowery herbage
yields:
Now blossom all the trees, and all the fields;

And all the woods their pomp of foliage wear,
And Nature's fairest robe adorns the blooming year.

Damoetas first th' alternate lay shall raise:
Th' inspiring Muses love alternate lays.

DAMOETAS.

Jove first I sing; ye Muses, aid my lay;
All nature owns his energy and sway;
The earth and heavens his sovereign bounty share,
And to my verses he vouchsafes his care.

MENALCAS.

With great Apollo I begin the strain,
For I am great Apollo's favourite swain;
For him the purple hyacinth I wear,
And sacred bay to Phoebus ever dear.

DAMOETAS.

The sprightly Galatea at my head
An apple flung, and to the willows fled;

But as along the level lawn she flew,
The wanton wish'd not to escape my view.

MENALCAS.

I LANGUISH'D long for fair AMYNTAS' charms,
But now he comes unbidden to my arms,
And with my dogs is so familiar grown,
That my own DELIA is no better known.

DAMOETAS.

I LATELY mark'd where midst the verdant shade
Two parent-doves had built their leafy bed;
I from the nest the young will shortly take,
And to my Love an handsome present make.

MENALCAS.

TEN ruddy wildings, from a lofty bough,
That through the green leaves beam'd with yellow glow,

I brought away, and to AMYNTAS bore;
Tomorrow I shall send as many more.

DAMOETAS.

AH the keen raptures! when my yielding
Fair
Breath'd her kind whispers to my ravish'd ear!
Waft, gentle gales, her accents to the skies,
That Gods themselves may hear with sweet surprise.

MENALCAS.

WHAT, though I am not wretched by your
scorn?
Say, beauteous boy, say can I cease to mourn,
If, while I hold the nets, the boar you face,
And rashly brave the dangers of the chace.

DAMOETAS.

SEND PHYLLIS home, IOLAS, for to-day
I celebrate my birth, and all is gay;

When for my crop the victim I prepare,
IOLAS in our festival may share.

MENALCAS.

PHYLLIS I love; she more than all can charm,
And mutual fires her gentle bosom warm:
Tears, when I leave her, bathe her beauteous eyes,
" A long, a long adieu, my Love!" she cries.

DAMOETAS.

THE wolf is dreadful to the wooly train,
Fatal to harvests is the crushing rain,
To the green woods the winds destructive prove,
To me the rage of mine offended Love.

MENALCAS.

THE willow's grateful to the pregnant ewes,
Showers to the corns, to kids the mountain-
      browse;
More grateful far to me my lovely boy,
In sweet AMYNTAS centers all my joy.

DAMOETAS.

Even Pollio deigns to hear my rural lays,
And chears the bashful Muse with generous praise;
Ye sacred Nine, for your great Patron feed
A beauteous heifer of the noblest breed.

MENALCAS.

Pollio the art of heavenly song adorns;
Then let a bull be bred with butting horns,
And ample front, that bellowing spurns the ground,
Tears up the turf, and throws the sands around.

DAMOETAS.

Him who my Pollio loves may nought annoy,
May he like Pollio every wish enjoy,
O may his happy lands with honey flow,
And on his thorns Assyrian roses blow!

MENALCAS.

Who hates not foolish BAVIUS, let him love
Thee, MÆVIUS, and thy tasteless rhymes approve!
Nor needs it thy admirer's reason shock
To milk the he-goats, and the foxes yoke.

DAMOETAS.

YE boys, on garlands who employ your care,
And pull the creeping strawberries, beware,
Fly for your lives, and leave that fatal place,
A deadly snake lies lurking in the grass.

MENALCAS.

FORBEAR, my flocks, and warily proceed,
Nor on that faithless bank securely tread;
The heedless ram late plung'd amid the pool,
And in the sun now dries his reeking wool.

DAMOETAS.

Ho TITYRUS! lead back the browsing flock,
And let them feed at distance from the brook;

At bathing-time I to the shade will bring
My goats, and wash them in the cooling spring.

MENALCAS.

Haste, from the sultry lawn the flocks remove
To the cool shelter of the shady grove:
When burning noon the curdling udder dries,
Th' ungrateful teats in vain the shepherd plies.

DAMOETAS.

How lean my bull in yonder mead appears,
Though the fat soil the richest pasture bears!
Ah Love! thou reign'st supreme in every heart,
Both flocks and shepherds languish with thy dart.

MENALCAS.

Love has not injur'd my consumptive flocks,
Yet bare their bones, and faded are their looks:
What envious eye hath squinted on my dams,
And sent its poison to my tender lambs!

DAMOETAS.

Say in what distant land the eye descries
But three short ells of all th' expanded skies;
Tell this, and great APOLLO be your name;
Your skill is equal, equal be your fame.

MENALCAS.

Say in what soil a wondrous flower is born,
Whose leaves the sacred names of kings adorn;
Tell this, and take my PHYLLIS to your arms,
And reign th' unrival'd sovereign of her charms.

PALÆMON.

'Tis not for me these high disputes to end;
Each to the heifer justly may pretend.
Such be their fortune, who so well can sing,
From love what painful joys, what pleasing torments spring.
Now, boys, obstruct the course of yonder rill,
The meadows have already drunk their fill.

THE FOURTH
PASTORAL.
POLLIO.

SICILIAN Muse, sublimer strains inspire,
And warm my bosom with diviner fire!
All take not pleasure in the rural scene,
In lowly tamarisks, and forests green.
If sylvan themes we sing, then let our lays
Deserve a CONSUL's ear, a CONSUL's praise.

> In this fourth Pastoral, no particular landscape is delineated. The whole is a prophetic song of triumph. But as almost all the images and allusions are of the rural kind, it is no less a true Bucolic than the others; if we admit the definition of a Pastoral, given us by an * Author of the first rank, who calls it " A poem in which any action or passion " is represented by its effects upon country life. "
>
> * The Author of the Rambler.

The age comes on, that future age of gold
In Cuma's myſtic prophecies foretold.
The Years begin their mighty courſe again,
The VIRGIN now returns, and the SATUR-
            NIAN reign.
Now from the lofty manſions of the ſky
To earth deſcends an heaven-born Progeny.
Thy PHOEBUS reigns, LUCINA, lend thine aid,
Nor be his birth his glorious birth delay'd!
An iron race ſhall then no longer rage,
But all the world regain the golden age.
This CHILD, the joy of nations, ſhall be born
Thy conſulſhip, O POLLIO, to adorn:

It is of little importance to enquire on what occaſion this poem was written. The ſpirit of prophetic enthuſiaſm that breathes through it, and the reſemblance it bears in many places to the Oriental manner, make it not improbable, that our Poet compoſed it partly from ſome pieces of antient prophecy that might have fallen into his hands, and that he afterwards inſcribed it to his friend and patron Pollio, on occaſion of the birth of his ſon Saloninus.

Thy confulfhip thefe happy times fhall prove,
And fee the mighty Months begin to move:
Then all our former guilt fhall be forgiv'n,
And man fhall dread no more th' avenging doom
  of heav'n.

The SON with heroes and with Gods fhall fhine,
And lead, enroll'd with them, the life divine.
He o'er the peaceful nations fhall prefide,
And his SIRE's virtues fhall his fceptre guide.
To thee, aufpicious BABE, th' unbidden earth
Shall bring the earlieft of her flowery birth;
Acanthus foft in fmiling beauty gay,
The bloffom'd bean, and ivy's flaunting fpray.
Th' untended goats fhall to their homes repair,
And to the milker's hand the loaded udder bear.
The mighty lion fhall no more be fear'd,
But graze innoxious with the friendly herd.

Sprung from thy cradle fragrant flowers shall
    spread,
And fanning bland shall wave around thy head.
Then shall the serpent die, with all his race:
No deadly herb the happy soil disgrace:
Assyrian balm on every bush shall bloom,
And breathe in every gale its rich perfume.
  But when thy FATHER's deeds thy youth shall
    fire,
And to great actions all thy soul inspire,
When thou shalt read of heroes and of kings,
And mark the glory that from virtue springs;
Then boundless o'er the far-extended plain
Shall wave luxuriant crops of golden grain,
With purple grapes the loaded thorn shall bend,
And streaming honey from the oak descend.
Nor yet old fraud shall wholly be effac'd;
Navies for wealth shall roam the watery waste;

Proud cities fenc'd with towery walls appear,
And cruel shares shall Earth's soft bosom tear:
Another TIPHYS o'er the swelling tide
With steady skill the bounding ship shall guide;
Another Argo with the flower of Greece
From Colchos' shore shall waft the golden fleece;
Again the world shall hear war's loud alarms,
And great ACHILLES shine again in arms.

 When riper years thy strengthen'd nerves shall brace,
And o'er thy limbs diffuse a manly grace,
The mariner no more shall plough the deep,
Nor load with foreign wares the trading ship,
Each country shall abound in every store,
Nor need the products of another shore.
Henceforth no plough shall cleave the fertile ground,
No pruninghook the tender vine shall wound;

The husbandman with toil no longer broke
Shall loose his ox for ever from the yoke.
No more the wool a foreign die shall feign,
But purple flocks shall graze the flowery plain,
Glittering in native gold the ram shall tread,
And scarlet lambs shall wanton on the mead.

In concord join'd with fate's unalter'd law
The Destinies these happy times foresaw,
They bade the sacred spindle swiftly run,
And hasten the auspicious ages on.

O dear to all thy kindred Gods above!
O Thou, the offspring of eternal JOVE!
Receive thy dignities, begin thy reign,
And o'er the world extend thy wide domain.
See nature's mighty frame exulting round,
Ocean, and earth, and heaven's immense profound!
See nations yet unborn with joy behold
Thy glad approach, and hail the age of gold!

O would th' Immortals lend a length of days,
And give a soul sublime to found thy praise;
Would Heaven this breast, this labouring breast inflame
With ardor equal to the mighty theme;
Not ORPHEUS with diviner transports glow'd,
When all her fire his Mother-muse bestow'd;
Nor loftier numbers flow'd from LINUS' tongue,
Although his sire APOLLO gave the song;
Even PAN, in presence of Arcadian swains
Would vainly strive to emulate my strains.

   Repay a Parent's care, O beauteous Boy,
And greet thy Mother with a smile of joy;
For thee, to loathing languors all resign'd
Ten slow-revolving months thy Mother pin'd.
* If cruel fate thy Parents bliss denies,
If no fond joy sits smiling in thine eyes,

---

   * If cruel fate &c.] This passage has perplexed all the Critics. Out of a number of significations that have been offered, the Transla-
tor

No nymph of heavenly birth shall crown thy love,

Nor shalt thou share th' immortal feasts above.

tor has pitched upon one, which he thinks the most agreable to the scope of the Poem and most consistent with the language of the original. The Reader, who wants more particulars on this head, may consult Servius, De La Cerda, or Ruæus.

THE FIFTH
PASTORAL.

MENALCAS, MOPSUS.

MENALCAS.

SINCE you with skill can touch the tuneful reed,
Since few my verses or my voice exceed;
In this refreshing shade shall we recline,
Where hasles with the lofty elms combine?

Here we discover Menalcas and Mopsus seated in an arbour formed by the interwoven twigs of a wild-vine. A grove of hasles and elms surrounds this arbour. The season seems to be summer. The time of the day is not specified.

MOPSUS.

Your riper age a due respect requires,
'Tis mine to yield to what my friend desires;
Whether you choose the zephyr's fanning breeze,
That shakes the wavering shadows of the trees;
Or the deep-shaded grotto's cool retreat:----
And see yon cave screen'd from the scorching heat,
Where the wild vine its curling tendrils weaves,
Whose grapes glow ruddy through the quivering leaves.

MENALCAS.

Of all the swains that to our hills belong,
Amyntas only vies with you in song.

MOPSUS.

What, though with me that haughty shepherd vie,
Who proudly dares Apollo's self defy?

MENALCAS.

Begin; let * Alcon's praise inspire your
strains,
Or Codrus' death, or Phyllis' amorous
pains;
Begin, whatever theme your Muse prefer.
To feed the kids be, Tityrus, thy care.

MOPSUS.

I rather will repeat that mournful song,
Which late I carv'd the verdant beeche along;
(I carv'd, and trill'd by turns the labour'd lay)
And let Amyntas match me if he may.

MENALCAS.

As slender willows where the olive grows,
Or sordid shrubs when near the scarlet rose,
Such (if the judgment I have form'd be true)
Such is Amyntas when compar'd with you.

* From this passage it is evident that Virgil thought Pastoral poetry capable of a much greater variety in its subjects, than some modern Critics will allow.

MOPSUS.

No more, MENALCAS; we delay too long,
The grot's dim shade invites my promis'd song.
  * When DAPHNIS fell by fate's remorseless
      blow,
The weeping nymphs pour'd wild the plaint of
      woe;
Witness, O hazle-grove, and winding stream,
  For all your echoes caught the mournful
      theme.
In agony of grief his Mother prest
The clay-cold carcase to her throbbing breast,
Frantic with anguish wail'd his hapless fate,
Rav'd at the stars, and heaven's relentless hate.

---

* When Daphnis] It is the most general and most probable conjecture, that Julius Cæsar is the Daphnis, whose death and deification are here celebrated. Some however are of opinion, that by Daphnis is meant a real shepherd of Sicily of that name, who is said to have invented Bucolic poetry, and in honour of whom the Sicilians performed yearly sacrifices.

'Twas then the swains in deep despair forsook

Their pining flocks, nor led them to the brook;

The pining flocks for him their pastures slight,

Nor grassy plains, nor cooling streams invite.

The doleful tidings reach'd the Libyan shores,

And lions mourn'd in deep repeated roars.

His cruel doom the woodlands wild bewail,

And plaintive hills repeat the melancholy tale.

'Twas he, who first Armenia's tygers broke,

And tam'd their stubborn natures to the yoke;

* He first with ivy wrapt the thyrsus round,

And made the hills with BACCHUS' rites resound,

As vines adorn the trees which they entwine,

As purple clusters beautify the vine,

As bulls the herd, as corns the fertile plains,

The godlike DAPHNIS dignified the swains.

* He first] This can be applied only to Julius Cæsar; for it was he who introduced at Rome the celebration of the Bacchanalian revels. SERVIUS.

When DAPHNIS from our eager hopes was torn,
PHOEBUS and PALES left the plains to mourn.
Now weeds and wretched tares the crop subdue,
Where store of generous wheat but lately grew.
Narcissus' lovely flower no more is seen,
No more the velvet violet decks the green;
Thistles for these the blasted meadow yields,
And thorns and frizled burs deform the fields.
Swains, shade the springs, and let the ground be drest
With verdant leaves; 'twas DAPHNIS' last request.
Erect a tomb in honour to his name
Mark'd with this verse to celebrate his fame.
‘ The swains with DAPHNIS' name this tomb
 ‘ adorn,
‘ Whose high renown above the skies is born;
‘ Fair was his flock, he fairest on the plain,
‘ The pride the glory of the sylvan reign.'

MENALCAS.

Sweeter, O bard divine, thy numbers seem,
Than to the scorched swain the cooling stream,
Or soft on fragrant flowrets to recline,
And the tir'd limbs to balmy sleep resign.
Blest youth! whose voice and pipe demand the praise
Due but to thine, and to thy master's lays.
I in return the darling theme will chuse,
And Daphnis' praises shall inspire my Muse;
He in my song shall high as heaven ascend,
High as the heavens, for Daphnis was my friend.

MOPSUS.

His virtues sure our noblest numbers claim;
Nought can delight me more than such a theme,
Which in your song new dignity obtains;
Oft has our Stimichon extol'd the strains.

MENALCAS.

Now DAPHNIS shines, among the Gods a God,
Struck with the splendors of his new abode.
Beneath his footstool far remote appear
The clouds slow-sailing, and the starry sphere.
Hence lawns and groves with gladsome raptures
    ring,
The swains, the nymphs, and PAN in concert sing.
The wolves to murder are no more inclin'd,
No guileful nets ensnare the wandering hind,
Deceit and violence and rapine cease,
For DAPHNIS loves the gentle arts of peace.
From savage mountains shouts of transport rise
Born in triumphant echoes to the skies;
The rocks and shrubs emit melodious sounds,
Through nature's vast extent THE GOD THE
    GOD rebounds.

Be gracious still, still present to our pray'r;
Four altars lo we build with pious care,
Two for th' inspiring God of song divine,
And two, propitious DAPHNIS, shall be thine.
Two bowls white-foaming with their milky store,
Of generous oil two brimming goblets more,
Each year we shall present before thy shrine,
And chear the feast with liberal draughts of wine;
Before the fire when winter-storms invade,
In summer's heat beneath the breezy shade.
The hallow'd bowls with wine of Chios crown'd
Shall pour their sparkling nectar to the ground.
DAMOETAS shall with * Lyctian ÆGON play,
And celebrate with festive strains the day:
ALPHESIBOEUS to the sprightly song
Shall like the dancing Satyrs trip along.
These rites shall still be paid, so justly due,
Both when the Nymphs receive our annual vow;

* Lyctium was a city of Crete.

And when with solemn songs, and victims crown'd,
Our lands in long procession we surround.
While fishes love the streams and briny deep,
And savage boars the mountain's rocky steep,
While grashoppers their dewy food delights,
While balmy thyme the busy bee invites;
So long shall last thine honours and thy fame,
So long the shepherds shall resound thy name.
Such rites to thee shall husbandmen ordain,
As CERES and the God of wine obtain.
Thou to our prayers propitiously inclin'd
Thy grateful suppliants to their vows shalt bind.

MOPSUS.

WHAT boon, dear shepherd, can your song
requite?
For nought in nature yields so sweet delight.
Not the soft sighing of the southern gale,
That faintly breathes along the flowery vale;

Nor, when light breezes curl the liquid plain,

To tread the margin of the murmuring main;

Nor melody of streams, that roll away

Through rocky dales, delights me as your lay.

MENALCAS.

No mean reward, my friend, your verses claim;

Take then this flute that breath'd the plaintive theme

Of * CORYDON; when proud ‡ DAMOETAS try'd

To match my skill, it dash'd his hasty pride.

MOPSUS.

And let this sheepcrook by my friend be worn,

Which brazen studs in beamy rows adorn;

This fair ANTIGENES oft beg'd to gain,

But all his beauty, all his prayers were vain.

* See Pastoral second.
‡ See Pastoral third.

THE

THE SIXTH

PASTORAL.

SILENUS.

MY sportive Muse first sung Sicilian strains,
Nor blush'd to dwell in woods and lowly plains.
To sing of kings and wars when I aspire,
APOLLO checks my vainly-rising fire.
' To swains the flock and sylvan pipe belong,
' Then choose some humbler theme, nor dare heroic song.'
The voice divine, O VARUS, I obey,
And to my reed shall chant a rural lay;

Since others long thy praises to rehearse,
And sing thy battles in immortal verse.
Yet if these songs, which PHOEBUS bids me write,
Hereafter to the swains shall yield delight,
Of thee the trees and humble shrubs shall sing,
And all the vocal grove with VARUS ring.
The song inscrib'd to VARUS' sacred name
To PHOEBUS' favour has the justest claim.

Come then, my Muse, a sylvan song repeat.
* 'Twas in his shady arbour's cool retreat
Two youthful swains the God SILENUS found,
In drunkenness and sleep his senses bound.
His turgid veins the late debauch betray;
His garland on the ground neglected lay,

---

* The cave of Silenus, which is the scene of this eclogue, is delineated with sufficient accuracy. The time seems to be the evening; at least the song does not cease, till the flocks are folded, and the evening star appears.

Fallen from his head; and by the well-worn ear
His cup of ample size depended near.
Sudden with swains the sleeping God surprise,
And with his garland bind him as he lies,
(No better chain at hand) incens'd so long
To be defrauded of their promis'd song.
To aid their project, and remove their fears,
ÆGLE a beauteous fountain-nymph appears;
Who, while he hardly opes his heavy eyes,
His stupid brow with bloody berries dies.
Then smiling at the fraud SILENUS said,
' And dare you thus a sleeping God invade?
' To see me was enough; but haste, unloose
' My bonds; the song no longer I refuse;
' Unloose me, youths; my song shall pay your
  ' pains;
' For this fair nymph another boon remains.'
 He sung; responsive to the heavenly sound
The stubborn oaks and forests dance around,

Tripping the Satyrs and the Fauns advance,
Wild beasts forget their rage, and join the general
dance.
Not so Parnassus' listening rocks rejoice,
When PHOEBUS raises his celestial voice;
Nor Thracia's echoing mountains so admire,
When ORPHEUS strikes the loud-lamenting
lyre.
For first he sung of Nature's wondrous birth;
How seeds of water, air, and flame, and earth,
Down the vast void with casual impulse hurl'd,
Clung into shapes, and form'd this fabric of the
world.
Then hardens by degrees the tender soil,
And from the mighty mound the seas recoil.
O'er the wide world new various forms arise;
The infant-sun along the brighten'd skies
Begins his course, while earth with glad amaze
The blazing wonder from below surveys.

The clouds sublime their genial moisture shed,
And the green grove lifts high its leafy head.
The savage beasts o'er desart mountains roam,
Yet few their numbers, and unknown their home.
He next the blest SATURNIAN ages sung;
How a new race of men from * PYRRHA
        sprung;
PROMETHEUS' daring theft, and dreadful doom,
Whose growing heart devouring birds consume.
Then names the spring renown'd for HYLAS'
        fate
By the sad mariners bewail'd too late;
They call on HYLAS with repeated cries,
And HYLAS, HYLAS, all the lonesome shore
        replies.
Next he bewails PASIPHAE (hapless dame!)
Who for a bullock felt a brutal flame.

T

---

* See Ovid Met. Lib. I.

What fury fires thy bosom, frantic queen!
How happy thou, if herds had never been!
The * Maids, whom JUNO, to avenge her wrong,
Like heifers doom'd to lowe the vales along,
Ne'er felt the rage of thy detested fire,
Ne'er were polluted with thy foul desire;
Though oft for horns they felt their polish'd brow,
And their soft necks oft fear'd the galling plough.
Ah wretched queen! thou roam'st the mountain-waste,
While, his white limbs on lillies laid to rest,
The half-digested herb again he chews,
Or some fair female of the herd pursues.
' Beset, ye Cretan nymphs, beset the grove,
' And trace the wandering footsteps of my love.

* Their names were Lysippe, Ipponoë, and Cyrianassa. Juno, to be avenged of them for preferring their own beauty to hers, struck them with madness, to such a degree, that they imaginined themselves to be heifers.

' Yet let my longing eyes my love behold,

' Before some favourite beauty of the fold

' Entice him with * Gortynian herds to stray,

' Where smile the vales in richer pasture gay.'

He sung how golden fruit's resistless grace

Decoy'd the † wary Virgin from the race.

‡ Then wraps in bark the mourning Sisters round,

And rears the lofty alders from the ground.

He sung, while GALLUS by § Permessus stray'd,

A Sister of the Nine the hero led

To the Aonian hill; the choir in haste

Left their bright thrones, and hail'd the welcome
          guest.

LINUS arose, for sacred song renown'd,

Whose brow a wreathe of flowers and parsley
          bound;

---

* Gortyna was a city of Crete. See Ovid. Art. Am. Lib. I.
† Atalanta. See Ovid. Metamorph. Lib. X.
‡ See Ovid. Met. Lib. II.
§ A river in Bœotia arising from mount Helicon, sacred to the Muses.

And, 'Take, he said, this pipe, which heretofore
' The far-fam'd * Shepherd of Ascræa bore;
' Then heard the mountain-oaks its magic sound,
' Leap'd from their hills, and thronging danced
'   around.
' On this thou shalt renew the tuneful lay,
' And grateful songs to thy APOLLO pay,
' Whose fam'd † Grynæan temple from thy strain
' Shall more exalted dignity obtain.'
Why should I sing unhappy ‡ SCYLLA's fate?
Sad monument of jealous CIRCE's hate!
Round her white breast what furious monsters
    roll,
And to the dashing waves incessant howl:
How from the § ships that bore ULYSSES' crew
Her dogs the trembling sailors drag'd, and slew.

* Hesiod.
† Grynium was a maritime town of the Lesser Asia, where were an antient temple and oracle of Apollo.
‡ See Virgil Æn. III.
§ See Homer Odyss. Lib. XII.

Of † PHILOMELA's feast why should I sing,
And what dire chance befel the Thracian king?
Changed to a lapwing by th' avenging God
He made the barren waste his lone abode,
And oft on soaring pinions hover'd o'er
The lofty palace then his own no more.

   The tuneful God renews each pleasing theme,
Which PHOEBUS sung by bless'd Eurotas' stream;
When bless'd Eurotas gently flow'd along,
And bade his laurels learn the lofty song.
SILENUS sung; the vocal vales reply,
And heavenly music charms the listening sky.
But now their folds the number'd flocks invite,
The star of evening sheds its trembling light,
And the unwilling heavens are wrapt in night.

† See Ovid's Metamorph. Lib. VI.

THE SEVENTH

PASTORAL.

MELIBOEUS, CORYDON, THYRSIS.

MELIBOEUS.

BENEATH an holm that murmur'd to the breeze
The youthful DAPHNIS lean'd in rural ease:
With him two gay Arcadian swains reclin'd,
Who in the neighbouring vale their flocks had join'd,

The scene of this Pastoral is as follows. Four shepherds, Daphnis in the most distinguished place, Corydon, Thyrsis and Meliboeus are seen reclining beneath an holm. Sheep and goats intermixed are feeding hard by. At a little distance Mincius fringed with reeds appears winding along. Fields and trees compose the surrounding scene. A venerable oak, with bees swarming around it, is particularly distinguished. The time seems to be the forenoon of a summer-day.

Thyrsis, whose care it was the goats to keep,
And Corydon, who fed the fleecy sheep;
Both in the flowery prime of youthful days,
Both skill'd in single or responsive lays.
While I with busy hand a shelter form
To guard my myrtles from the future storm,
The husband of my goats had chanced to stray:
To find the vagrant out I take my way.
Which Daphnis seeing cries, ' Dismiss your
   ' fear,
' Your kids and goat are all in safety here;
' And, if no other care require your stay,
' Come, and with us unbend the toils of day
' In this cool shade; at hand your heifers feed,
' And of themselves will to the watering speed;
' Here fringed with reeds flow Mincius winds
   ' along,
' And round yon oak the bees soft-murmuring
   ' throng.'

What could I do? for I was left alone,

My PHYLLIS and ALCIPPE both were gone,

And none remain'd to feed my weanling lambs,

And to restrain them from their bleating dams:

Betwixt the swains a solemn match was set,

To prove their skill, and end a long debate.

Though serious matters claim'd my due regard,

Their pastime to my business I prefer'd.

To sing by turns the Muse inspir'd the swains,

And CORYDON began th' alternate strains.

CORYDON.

YE Nymphs of Helicon, my sole desire!

O warm my breast with all my CODRUS' fire.

If none can equal CODRUS' heavenly lays,

For next to PHOEBUS he deserves the praise,

No more I ply the tuneful art divine,

My silent pipe shall hang on yonder pine.

THYRSIS.

ARCADIAN swains, an ivy wreathe bestow,
With early honours crown your poet's brow;
CODRUS shall chafe, if you my songs commend,
Till burning spite his tortur'd entrails rend;
Or amulets, to bind my temples, frame,
Lest his invidious praises blast my fame.

CORYDON.

A STAG's tall horns, and stain'd with savage gore
This bristled visage of a tusky boar,
To thee, O Virgin-goddess of the chace,
Young MYCON offers for thy former grace.
If like success his future labours crown,
Thine, Goddess, then shall be a nobler boon,
In polish'd marble thou shalt shine complete,
And purple sandals shall adorn thy feet.

THYRSIS.

To thee, *PRIAPUS, each returning year,
This bowl of milk, these hallow'd cakes we bear;
Thy care our garden is but meanly stor'd,
And mean oblations all we can afford.
But if our flocks a numerous offspring yield,
And our decaying fold again be fill'd,
Though now in marble thou obscurely shine,
For thee a golden statue we design.

CORYDON.

O GALATEA, whiter than the swan,
Loveliest of all thy sisters of the main,
Sweeter than Hybla, more than lillies fair!
If ought of CORYDON employ thy care,
When shades of night involve the silent sky,
And slumbering in their stalls the oxen lie,
Come to my longing arms, and let me prove
Th' immortal sweets of GALATEA's love.

* This Deity presided over gardens.

THYRSIS.

As the vile sea-weed scatter'd by the storm,
As he whose face * Sardinian herbs deform,
As burs and brambles that disgrace the plain,
So nauseous so detested be thy swain;
If when thine absence I am doom'd to bear
The day appears not longer than a year.
Go home, my flocks, ye lengthen out the day,
For shame, ye tardy flocks, for shame away!

CORYDON.

Ye mossy fountains warbling as ye flow!
And softer than the slumbers ye bestow
Ye grassy banks! ye trees with verdure crown'd,
Whose leaves a glimmering shade diffuse around!
Grant to my weary flocks a cool retreat,
And screen them from the summer's raging heat;

---

* It was the property of this poisonous herb to distort the features of those who had eaten of it, in such a manner, that they seemed to expire in an agony of laughter.

For now the year in brighteſt glory ſhines,
Now reddening cluſters deck the bending vines.

THYRSIS.

Here's wood for fuel; here the fire diſplays
To all around its animating blaze;
Black with continual ſmoke our poſts appear;
Nor dread we more the rigour of the year,
Than the fell wolf the fearful lambkins dreads,
When he the helpleſs fold by night invades;
Or ſwelling torrents, headlong as they roll,
The weak reſiſtance of the ſhatter'd mole.

CORYDON.

Now yellow harveſts wave on every field,
Now bending boughs the hoary cheſnut yield,
Now loaded trees reſign their annual ſtore,
And on the ground the mellow fruitage pour;
Jocund the face of Nature ſmiles, and gay;
But if the fair ALEXIS were away,

Inclement drought the hardening soil would
 drain,
And streams no longer murmur o'er the plain.

THYRSIS.

A LANGUID hue the thirsty fields assume,
Parch'd to the root the flowers resign their bloom,
The faded vines refuse their hills to shade,
Their leafy verdure wither'd and decay'd;
But if my PHYLLIS on these plains appear,
Again the groves their gayest green shall wear,
Again the clouds their copious moisture lend,
And in the genial rain shall JOVE descend.

CORYDON.

ALCIDES' brows the poplar-leaves surround,
APOLLO's beamy locks with bays are crown'd,
The myrtle, lovely Queen of smiles, is thine,
And jolly BACCHUS loves the curling vine;
But while my PHYLLIS loves the hazle-spray,
To hazle yield the myrtle and the bay.

THYRSIS.

The fir, the hills; the ash adorns the woods;
The pine, the gardens; and the poplar, floods.
If thou, my LYCIDAS, wilt deign to come,
And chear thy shepherd's solitary home,
The ash so fair in woods, and garden-pine
Will own their beauty far excel'd by thine.

MELIBOEUS.

So sung the swains, but THYRSIS strove in vain;
Thus far I bear in mind th' alternate strain.
Young CORYDON acquir'd unrival'd fame,
And still we pay a deference to his name.

THE EIGHTH

PASTORAL.

DAMON, ALPHESIBOEUS.

Rehearse we, Pollio, the enchant-
　　　　ing strains
Alternate sung by two contending swains.
Charm'd by their songs, the hungry heifers stood
In deep amaze, unmindful of their food;
The listening lynxes laid their rage aside,
The streams were silent, and forgot to glide.

In this eight Pastoral no particular scene is described. The Poet rehearses the songs of two contending swains Damon and Alphesibœus. The former adopts the soliloquy of a despairing lover: the latter chooses for his subject the magic rites of an Enchantress forsaken by her lover, and recalling him by the power of her spells.

O Thou, where'er thou lead'st thy conquering host,
Or by * Timavus, or th' Illyrian coast!
When shall my Muse transported with the theme
In strains sublime my POLLIO's deeds proclaim;
And celebrate thy lays by all admir'd,
Such as of old SOPHOCLES' Muse inspir'd?
To thee, the patron of my rural songs,
To thee my first my latest lay belongs.
Then let this humble ivy-wreathe inclose,
Twin'd with triumphal bays, thy godlike brows.

 What time the chill sky brightens with the dawn,
When cattle love to crop the dewy lawn,
Thus DAMON to the woodlands wild complain'd,
As 'gainst an olive's lofty trunk he lean'd.

DAMON.

LEAD on the genial day, O Star of morn!
While wretched I, all hopeless and forlorn,

---

* A river in Italy.

With my laſt breath my fatal woes deplore,
And call the Gods by whom falſe NISA ſwore;
Though they, regardleſs of a lover's pain,
Heard her repeated vows, and heard in vain.
* Begin, my pipe, the ſweet Mænalian ſtrain.

Bleſt Mænalus! that hears the paſtoral ſong
Still languiſhing its tuneful groves along!
That hears th' Arcadian God's celeſtial lay,
Who taught the idly-ruſtling reeds to play!
That hears the ſinging pines! that hears the ſwain
Of love's ſoft chains melodiouſly complain!
Begin, my pipe, the ſweet Mænalian ſtrain.

MOPSUS the willing NISA now enjoys——
What may not lovers hope from ſuch a choice!

X

---

* This *intercalary line* (as it called by the Commentators) which ſeems to be intended as a chorus or burden to the ſong, is here made the laſt of a triplet, that it may be as independent of the context and the verſe in the tranſlation, as it is in the Original.——Mænalus was a mountain of Arcadia.

Now mares and griffins shall their hate resign,
And the succeeding age shall see them join
In friendship's tie; now mutual love shall bring
The dog and doe to share the friendly spring.
Scatter thy nuts, O MOPSUS, and prepare
The nuptial torch to light the wedded Fair.
Lo Hesper hastens to the western main!
And thine the night of bliss---thine, happy swain!
Begin, my pipe, the sweet Mænalian strain.

 Exult, O NISA, in thy happy state!
Supremely blest in such a worthy mate!
While you my beard detest, and bushy brow,
And think the gods forget the world below:
While you my flock and rural pipe disdain,
And treat with bitter scorn a faithful swain.
Begin, my pipe, the sweet Mænalian strain.

When first I saw you by your mother's side,
To where our apples grew I was your guide:
Twelve summers since my birth had roll'd a-
    round,
And I could reach the branches from the ground.
How did I gaze!---how perish!---ah how vain
The fond bewitching hopes that sooth'd my
    pain!
Begin, my pipe, the sweet Mænalian strain.

   Too well I know thee, LOVE. From Scy-
    thian snows,
Or Lybia's burning sands the mischief rose.
Rocks adamantine nurs'd this foreign bane,
This fell invader of the peaceful plain.
Begin, my pipe, the sweet Mænalian strain.

   Love taught the * Mother's murdering hand
    to kill,
Her children's blood Love bade the Mother spill.

* Medea.

† Was Love the cruel cause? Or did the deed
From fierce unfeeling cruelty proceed?
Both fill'd her brutal bosom with their bane;
Both urg'd the deed, while Nature shrunk in vain.
Begin, my pipe, the sweet Mænalian strain.

Now let the fearful lamb the wolf devour;
Let alders blossom with Narcissus' flower;
From barren shrubs let radiant amber flow;
Let rugged oaks with golden fruitage glow;
Let shrieking owls with swans melodious vie;
Let TITYRUS the Thracian numbers try,
Outrival ORPHEUS in the sylvan reign,
And emulate ARION on the main.
Begin, my pipe, the sweet Mænalian strain.

---

† This seems to be Virgil's meaning. The Translator did not choose to preserve the conceit on the words *puer* and *mater* in his version; as this (in his opinion) would have rendered the passage obscure and unpleasing to an English reader.

Let land no more the swelling waves divide;
Earth, be thou whelm'd beneath the boundless
tide;
Headlong from yonder promontory's brow
I plunge into the rolling deep below.
Farewell, ye woods! farewell, thou flowery plain!
Hear the last lay of a despairing swain.
And cease, my pipe, the sweet Mænalian strain.

   Here DAMON ceas'd. And now, ye tuneful
Nine,
ALPHESIBOEUS' magic verse subjoin.
To his responsive song your aid we call,
Our power extends not equally to all.

ALPHESIBOEUS.

   BRING living waters from the silver stream,
With vervain and fat incense feed the flame,
With this soft wreathe the sacred altars bind;
To move my cruel DAPHNIS to be kind,

And with my phrenzy to inflame his soul;
Charms are but wanting to complete the whole.
Bring DAPHNIS home, bring DAPHNIS to
                my arms,
O bring my long-loft love, my powerful charms.
  BY powerful charms what prodigies are done!
Charms draw pale CYNTHIA from her silver
                throne;
Charms burst the bloated snake, and * CIRCE's
                guests
By mighty magic charms were changed to beasts.
Bring DAPHNIS home, bring DAPHNIS to
                my arms,
O bring my long-loft love, my powerful charms.
  Three woolen wreathes, and each of triple die,
Three times about thy image I apply,

* See Hom. Odyff. Lib. X.

Then thrice I bear it round the sacred shrine;
Uneven numbers please the Powers divine.
Bring DAPHNIS home, bring DAPHNIS to
      my arms,
O bring my long-lost love, my powerful charms.
  Haste, let three colours with three knots be
      join'd,
And say, 'Thy fetters, VENUS, thus I bind.'
Bring DAPHNIS home, bring DAPHNIS to
      my arms,
O bring my long-lost love, my powerful charms.
  As this soft clay is harden'd by the flame,
And as this wax is soften'd by the same,
My love, that harden'd DAPHNIS to disdain,
Shall soften his relenting heart again.
Scatter the salted corn, and place the bays,
And with fat brimstone light the sacred blaze.

DAPHNIS my burning passion slights with scorn,
And DAPHNIS in this blazing bay I burn.
Bring DAPHNIS home, bring DAPHNIS to my arms,
O bring my long-lost love, my powerful charms.
As when, to find her love, an heifer roams
Through trackless groves, and solitary glooms;
Sick with desire, abandon'd to her woes,
By some lone stream her languid limbs she throws;
There in deep anguish wastes the tedious night,
Nor thoughts of home her late return invite:
Thus may he love, and thus indulge his pain,
While I enhance his torments with disdain.
Bring DAPHNIS home, bring DAPHNIS to my arms,
O bring my long-lost love, my powerful charms.

These robes beneath the threshold here I leave,
These pledges of his love, O earth, receive.
Ye dear memorials of our mutual fire,
Of you my faithless DAPHNIS I require.
Bring DAPHNIS home, bring DAPHNIS to
      my arms,
O bring my long-lost love, my powerful charms.

    These deadly poisons, and these magic weeds,
Selected from the store which Pontus breeds,
Sage MOERIS gave me; oft I saw him prove
Their sovereign power; by these, along the grove
A prowling wolf the dread magician roams;
Now gliding ghosts from the profoundest tombs
Inspir'd he calls; the rooted corn he wings,
And to strange fields the flying harvest brings.
Bring DAPHNIS home, bring DAPHNIS to
      my arms,
O bring my long-lost love, my powerful charms.

These ashes from the altar take with speed,
And treading backwards cast them o'er your head
Into the running stream, nor turn your eye.
Yet this last spell, though hopeless, let me try.
But nought can move the unrelenting swain,
And spells, and magic verse, and Gods are vain.
Bring DAPHNIS home, bring DAPHNIS to my arms,
O bring my long-lost love, my powerful charms.

 Lo, while I linger, with spontaneous fire
The ashes redden, and the flames aspire!
May this new prodigy auspicious prove!
What fearful hopes my beating bosom move!
Hark, does not Hylax bark!---ye Powers supreme,
Can it be real, or do lovers dream!---
He comes, my DAPHNIS comes; forbear my charms;
My love, my DAPHNIS flies to bliss my longing arms.

THE

THE NINTH

PASTORAL.

LYCIDAS, MOERIS.

LYCIDAS.

GO you to town, my friend? this beaten way
Conducts us thither.

MOERIS.

     Ah! the fatal day,
The unexpected day at last is come,
When a rude alien drives us from our home.

This and the first eclogue seem to have been written on the same occasion.—The time is a still evening. The landscape is described at the 97th line of this translation. On one side of the highway is an artificial arbour, where Lycidas invites Mœris to rest a
little

Hence, hence, ye clowns, th' usurper thus commands,
To me you must resign your antient lands.
Thus helpless and forlorn we yield to fate;
And our rapacious lord to mitigate
This brace of kids a present I design,
Which load with curses, O ye Powers divine!

LYCIDAS.

'Twas said, MENALCAS with his tuneful strains
Had sav'd the grounds of all the neighbouring swains,

little from the fatigue of his journey : and at a considerable distance appears a sepulchre by the way-side, where the antient sepulchres were commonly erected.

The Critics with one voice seem to condemn this eclogue as unworthy of its Author; I know not for what good reason. The many beautiful lines scattered through it would, one might think, be no weak recommendation. But it is by no means to be reckoned a loose collection of incoherent fragments; its principal parts are all strictly connected, and refer to a certain end, and its allusions and images are wholly suited to pastoral life. Its subject though uncommon is not improper: for what is more natural, than that two shepherds

From where the hill, that terminates the vale,

In easy risings first begins to swell,

Far as the blasted beeche that mates the sky,

And the clear stream that gently murmurs by.

MOERIS.

Such was the voice of fame; but music's charms,

Amid the dreadful clang of warlike arms,

Avail no more, than the Chaonian dove,

When down the sky descends the bird of JOVE.

And had not the prophetic raven spoke

His dire presages from the hollow oak,

And often warn'd me to avoid debate,

And with a patient mind submit to fate,

Ne'er had thy MOERIS seen this fatal hour,

And that melodious swain had been no more.

shepherds, when occasionally mentioning the good qualities of their absent friend, particularly his poetical talents, should repeat such fragments of his songs as they recollected?

LYCIDAS.

WHAT horrid breast such impious thoughts
could breed!
What barbarous hand could make MENALCAS
bleed!
Could every tender Muse in him destroy,
And from the shepherds ravish all their joy!
For who but he the lovely nymphs could sing,
Or paint the vallies with the purple spring?
Who shade the fountains from the glare of day?
Who but MENALCAS could compose the lay,
Which, as we journey'd to my love's abode,
I softly sung to chear the lonely road?
' * TITYRUS, while I am absent, feed the flock,
' And having fed conduct them to the brook,

---

* Tityrus] These lines, which Virgil has translated literally from Theocritus, may be supposed to be a fragment of the poem mentioned in the preceeding verses; or, what is more likely, to be spoken by Lycidas to his servant; something similar to which may be seen Past. 5. v. 20. of this translation:—The Original is here remarkably explicit, even to a degree of affectation. This the Translator has endeavoured to imitate.

' (The way is short, and I shall soon return)
' But shun the he-goat with the butting horn.'

MOERIS.

Or who could finish the imperfect lays
Sung by MENALCAS to his VARUS' praise?
' If fortune yet shall spare the Mantuan swains,
' And save from plundering hands our peaceful
    ' plains,
' Nor doom us sad Cremona's fate to share,
' (For ah! a neighbour's woe excites our fear)
' Then high as heaven our VARUS' fame shall
    ' rise,
' The warbling swans shall bear it to the skies.'

LYCIDAS.

Go on, dear swain, these pleasing songs pursue;
So may thy bees avoid the bitter yew,
So may rich herds thy fruitful fields adorn,
So may thy cows with strutting dugs return.

Even I with poets have obtain'd a name,
The Muse inspires me with poetic flame;
Th' applauding shepherds to my songs attend,
But I suspect my skill, though they commend.
I dare not hope to please a CINNA's ear,
Or sing what VARUS might vouchsafe to hear.
Harsh are the sweetest lays that I can bring,
So screams a goose where swans melodious sing.

MOERIS.

THIS I am pondering, if I can rehearse
The lofty numbers of that labour'd verse.
' Come, GALATEA, leave the rolling seas;
' Can rugged rocks and heaving surges please?
' Come, taste the pleasures of our sylvan bowers,
' Our balmy-breathing gales, and fragrant flowers.
' See, how our plains rejoice on every side,
' How crystal streams through blooming vallies
   ' glide:

'O'er the cool grot the whitening poplars bend,
'And clasping vines their grateful umbrage lend.
'Come, beauteous nymph, forsake the briny wave,
'Loud on the beach let the wild billows rave.'

LYCIDAS.

Or what you sung one evening on the plain—
The air, but not the words, I yet retain.

MOERIS.

'Why, Daphnis, dost thou calculate the
   'skies,
'To know when antient constellations rise?
'Lo, Cæsar's star its radiant light displays,
'And on the nations sheds propitious rays.
'On the glad hills the reddening clusters glow,
'And smiling Plenty decks the plains below.
'Now graff thy pears; the star of Cæsar reigns,
'To thy remotest race the fruit remains.'

The rest I have forgot, for length of years
Deadens the sense, and memory impairs.
All things in time submit to sad decay;
Oft have we sung whole summer suns away.
These vanish'd joys must MOERIS now deplore,
His voice delights, his numbers charm no more;
* Him have the wolves beheld, bewitch'd his song,
Bewitch'd to silence his melodious tongue.
But your desire MENALCAS can fulfil,
All these, and more, he sings with matchless skill.

LYCIDAS.

THESE faint excuses which my MOERIS frames
But heighten my desire.---And now the streams
In slumber-soothing murmurs softly flow;
And now the sighing breeze hath ceas'd to blow.

---

* In Italia creditur luporum visus esse noxios; vocemque homini quem priores contemplentur adimere ad præsens.
Plin. N. H. VIII. 22.

Half of our way is paſt, for I deſcry
* BIANOR's tomb juſt riſing to the eye.
Here in this leafy arbour eaſe your toil,
Lay down your kids, and let us ſing the while:
We ſoon ſhall reach the town; or, leſt a ſtorm
Of ſudden rain the evening-ſky deform,
Be yours to chear the journey with a ſong,
Eas'd of your load, which I ſhall bear along.

MÓERIS.

No more, my friend; your kind entreaties ſpare,
And let our journey be our preſent care;
Let fate reſtore our abſent friend again,
Then gladly I reſume the tuneful ſtrain.

---

* Bianor is ſaid to have founded Mantua.   SERVIUS.

THE TENTH

PASTORAL.

GALLUS.

TO my laft labour lend thy facred aid,
O Arethusa: that the cruel Maid

The fcene of this Paftoral is very accurately delineated. We behold the forlorn Gallus ftretched along beneath a folitary cliff, his flocks ftanding round him at fome diftance. A groupe of deities and fwains encircle him, each of whom is particularly defcribed. On one fide we fee the fhepherds with their crooks; next to them the neatherds known by the clumfinefs of their appearance; and next to thefe Menalcas with his clothes wet, as juft come from beating or gathering winter-maft. On the other fide we obferve Apollo with his ufual infignia; Sylvanus crown'd with flowers and brandifhing in his hand the long lillies and flowering fennel; and laft of all Pan, the god of fhepherds, known by his ruddy fmiling countenance, and the other peculiarities of his form.

Gallus was a Roman of very confiderable rank, a poet of no fmall eftimation, and an intimate friend of Virgil. He loved to diftraction one Cytheris (here called Lycoris) who flighted him, and followed Antony into Gaul.

With deep remorse may read the mournful song,
For mournful lays to GALLUS' love belong.
(What Muse in sympathy will not bestow
Some tender strains to soothe my GALLUS' woe?)
So may thy waters pure of briny stain
Traverse the waves of the Sicilian main.
Sing, mournful Muse, of GALLUS' luckless love,
While the goats browse along the cliffs above.
Nor silent is the waste while we complain,
The woods return the long-resounding strain.

 Whither, ye fountain-Nymphs, were ye withdrawn,
To what lone woodland, or what devious lawn,
When GALLUS' bosom languish'd with the fire
Of hopeless love, and unallay'd desire?
For neither by th' Aonian spring you stray'd,
Nor roam'd Parnassus' heights, nor Pindus' hallow'd shade.

The pines of Mænalus were heard to mourn,
And sounds of woe along the groves were born.
And sympathetic tears the laurel shed,
  And humbler shrubs declin'd their drooping
      head.
All wept his fate, when to despair resign'd
Beneath a desart-cliff he lay reclin'd.
Lyceus' rocks were hung with many a tear,
And round the swain his flocks forlorn appear.
Nor scorn, celestial bard, a Poet's name;
Renown'd ADONIS by the lonely stream
Tended his flock.---As thus he lay along,
The swains and awkward neatherds round him
      throng.
Wet from the winter-mast MENALCAS came.
All ask, what Beauty rais'd the fatal flame.
The God of verse vouchsafed to join the rest;
He said, What phrensy thus torments thy breast?

While she, thy darling, thy LYCORIS scorns
Thy proffer'd love, and for another burns,
With whom o'er winter-wastes she wanders far,
'Midst camps, and clashing arms, and boisterous war.
SYLVANUS came with rural garlands crown'd,
And wav'd the lillies long, and flowering fennel round.
Next we beheld the gay Arcadian God;
His smiling cheeks with bright vermilion glow'd.
For ever wilt thou heave the bursting sigh?
Is Love regardful of the weeping eye?
Love is not cloy'd with tears; alas, no more
Than bees luxurious with the balmy flow'r,
Than goats with foliage, than the grassy plain
With silver rills and soft refreshing rain.
PAN spoke; and thus the Youth with grief opprest;
Arcadians, hear, O hear my last request;

O ye, to whom the sweetest lays belong,
O let my sorrows on your hills be sung:
If your soft flutes shall celebrate my woes,
How will my bones in deepest peace repose!
Ah had I been with you a country-swain,
And prun'd the vine, and fed the bleating train;
Had PHYLLIS, or some other rural Fair,
Or black AMYNTAS been my darling care;
(Beauteous though black; what lovelier flower is
  seen
Than the dark violet on the painted green?)
These in the bower had yielded all their charms,
And sunk with mutual raptures in my arms;
PHYLLIS had crown'd my head with garlands
  gay,
AMYNTAS sung the pleasing hours away.
Here, O LYCORIS, purls the limpid spring,
Bloom all the meads, and all the woodlands sing;

Here let me preſs thee to my panting breaſt,
Till youth, and joy, and life itſelf be paſt.
Baniſh'd by love o'er hoſtile lands I ſtray,
And mingle in the battle's dread array;
Whilſt thou, relentleſs to my conſtant flame,
(Ah could I diſbelieve the voice of Fame!)
Far from thy home, unaided and forlorn,
Far from thy love, thy faithful love, art born,
On the bleak Alps with chilling blaſts to pine,
Or wander waſte along the frozen Rhine.
Ye icy paths, O ſpare her tender form!
O ſpare thoſe heavenly charms, thou wintry ſtorm!

Hence let me haſten to ſome deſart-grove,
And ſoothe with ſongs my long-unanſwer'd love.
I go, in ſome lone wilderneſs to ſuit
Eubœan lays to my Sicilian flute.
Better with beaſts of prey to make abode
In the deep cavern, or the darkſome wood;

And carve on trees the ſtory of my woe,
Which with the growing bark ſhall ever grow.
Meanwhile with woodland-nymphs, a lovely throng,
The winding groves of Mænalus along
I roam at large; or chace the foaming boar;
Or with ſagacious hounds the wilds explore,
Careleſs of cold. And now methinks I bound
O'er rocks and cliffs, and hear the woods reſound;
And now with beating heart I ſeem to wing
The Cretan arrow from the Parthian ſtring----
As if I thus my phrenſy could forego,
As if love's God could melt at human woe.
Alas! nor nymphs nor heavenly ſongs delight---
Farewell, ye groves! the groves no more invite.
No pains no miſeries of man can move
The unrelenting Deity of love.

To quench your thirst in Hebrus' frozen flood,
To make the Scythian snows your drear abode;
Or feed your flock on Aethiopian plains,
When Sirius' fiery constellation reigns,
(When deep-imbrown'd the languid herbage lies,
And in the elm the vivid verdure dies)
Were all in vain. LOVE's unresisted sway
Extends to all, and we must LOVE obey.

 'Tis done; ye NINE, here ends your poet's strain
In pity sung to soothe his GALLUS' pain.
While leaning on a flowery bank I twine
The flexile osiers, and the basket join.
Celestial NINE, your sacred influence bring,
And soothe my GALLUS' sorrows while I sing:
GALLUS, my much-belov'd! for whom I feel
The flame of purest friendship rising still:

So by a brook the verdant alders rife,
When fostering zephyrs fan the vernal skies.

Let us be gone: at eve, the shade annoys
With noxious damps, and hurts the singer's voice,
The juniper breathes bitter vapours round,
That kill the springing corn, and blast the ground.
Homeward, my sated goats, now let us hie;
Lo beamy Hesper gilds the western sky.

THE END.

THE
JUDGMENT
OF
PARIS.

A POEM.

By JAMES BEATTIE, M. A.

ἌΜΑΧΟΝ ΔΈ ΚΡΎΨΑΙ ΤΟ῾ ΣΥΓΓΕΝΕ῾Σ Ἦ͂ΘΟΣ·
PINDAR. OLYMP. 13.

LONDON:
Printed for T. BECKET and P. A. DE HONDT, at Tully's Head, in the Strand; and J. BALFOUR, in Edinburgh.
M DCC LXV.

[Price One Shilling and Six-pence.]

PREFACE.

IF all the powers of human nature could be gratified at once, such an universal gratification would certainly constitute the Supreme Felicity of man. But this is impossible: for our appetites and affections are in many instances incompatible; and whatever course of life we pursue, we must forego some gratifications, if we would hope to attain others. Self-denial is not peculiar to the virtuous; the sensualist and the ruffian cannot exempt themselves from it. But virtuous self-denial restrains only those propensities, whose influence is most limited, and which, when indulged, introduce disorder into the mind; whereas, that abstinence which the vitious impose upon themselves, restrains the noblest and most important principles of their nature, and such as are of the most extensive influence: the latter doth necessarily contract our sphere of enjoyment, and the former doth as necessarily enlarge it.

After an accurate induction of particulars, it hath been shewn by Moral Writers, with a degree of evidence, which, if it cannot be called strict demonstration, is at least sufficient to command the assent of every reasonable man, that Virtue hath a natural tendency to produce, and is perfectly consistent with, the amplest and most diffusive gratification of our *Whole Nature*. The pursuit of *Ambition*, or of *Sensual Pleasure*, can promise only *partial* happiness; being adapted, not to our *whole* constitution, but only to a *part* of it. The propensities, which determine us to such pursuits, are certainly Natural propensities; and as such, when separately considered, may seem conducive to the perfection of human felicity: a consideration, upon which the Sensual and the Ambitious found a plea, that often appears specious, and often proves ensnaring. But pleasures cannot be properly estimated when *separately* considered: we ought to estimate them according to their comparative excellence, and according to their influence on the General happiness of the *Whole mental system*.

The following Essay is to be looked upon as an attempt to illustrate some points of this important doctrine. The Fable, from which it derives its name, its scenery, and principal incidents, is well known; and is, indeed, in its original state, no very proper vehicle for communicating any moral doctrine: but, after changing some circumstances, omitting others, and retaining such only as were necessary for embellishing the sentiments,

ments, and rendering the cataſtrophe probable, I thought it more favourable to my deſign, than any that I could have invented. The rule which Horace hath ſuggeſted in theſe lines,

> Rectius Iliacum carmen deducis in actus,
> Quam ſi proferres ignota indictaque primus:

will perhaps appear as applicable to ſmall as to great works.

Some will doubtleſs think it abſurd, to introduce any part of the Pagan, or rather Homeric Theology, into a modern poem profeſſedly ſerious. But the attentive Reader will perceive, that the celeſtial Beings introduced into this poem, whom the ſubject rendered it neceſſary to diſtinguiſh by the names of Juno, Pallas, and Venus, repreſent, not the characters of theſe goddeſſes as we find them in Homer, but only ſuch characters, as the Patroneſſes of *Ambition*, of *Wiſdom*, and of *Effeminate Pleaſure*, might be ſuppoſed to aſſume. The arguments or topicks, by which their ſeveral doctrines are enforced, are all deduced from the principles of human nature. But they differ eſſentially in this reſpect; the arguments of the Firſt Speaker and of the Laſt proceed from *Partial* views of our frame; thoſe of the Second, from a view of the *Whole* as conſtituting one ſyſtem.

It

It is hoped, the character of Paris, as here represented, will be found strictly agreeable to the idea of him conveyed to us in the writings of Homer, and other antient poets. The probability of the cataſtrophe depends very much on the Real Character of this perſonage; and therefore, with regard to him, a cloſe adherence to Poetic Truth was judged altogether neceſſary.

It will not perhaps be improper to obſerve, that as the following Compoſition was intended to partake no leſs of the Lyric than of the Heroic ſtyle, I have therefore made choice of that ſpecies of verſification, which to me ſeems equally ſuſceptible of both; and which, in the judgment of Mr. DRYDEN*, is " More noble, and " of greater dignity, both for the ſound and number," than any other regular ſtanza of Engliſh verſe.

September 5, 1764.

* Preface to *Annus Mirabilis*, printed 1667.

THE

THE

JUDGMENT OF PARIS.

FAR in the depth of Ida's inmoſt grove,
    That faintly murmur'd to the vernal wind;
Where flowery woodbines wild by Nature wove
    Form'd the lone bower, THE ROYAL SWAIN reclin'd.

Up the broad cliffs, that tower'd immenſe to heaven,
    Green waved the lofty pines, on every ſide,
Save where, fair-opening to the beam of even,
    A dale ſloped gradual to the valley wide.

Echoed the vale with many a chearful note;
 The various lowe of herds refounding long,
The fhrilling pipe, the mellow horn remote,
 And focial clamours of the feftive throng.

For now, low-hovering o'er the weftern main,
 Where amber clouds begirt his dazzling throne,
The fun with ruddier verdure deck'd the plain;
 And lakes, and ftreams, and fpires triumphal fhone;

And many a band of ardent youths were feen:
 Some, into rapture fired by glory's charms,
Or hurl'd the thundering car along the green,
 Or march'd embattled on in glittering arms.

Others more mild, in happy leifure gay,
 The winding foreft's lonely gloom explore;
Or by Scamander's flowery margin ftray,
 Or the blue Hellefpont's refounding fhore.

But

But chief the eye to Ilion's glories turn'd,
  That gleam'd along th' extended champaign far;
And bulwarks, in terrific pomp adorn'd,
  Where Peace sat smiling at the frowns of War.

Rich in the spoils of many a subject-clime
  In pride luxurious blazed th' imperial dome;
Tower'd mid th' encircling grove the fane sublime;
  And dread memorials mark'd the hallow'd tomb

Of Him, who from the gore-stain'd cavern led
  The savage stern, and sooth'd his boisterous breast;
Who spoke, and Science rear'd her radiant head,
  And brighten'd o'er the long-benighted waste;

Or, greatly daring in his country's cause,
  Whose heaven-taught soul the aweful plan design'd,
Whence Power stood trembling at the voice of Laws,
  Whence soar'd on Freedom's wing th' ethereal mind.

But not the pomp that Royalty displays,
 Not all th' imperial pride of lofty Troy,
Nor Virtue's triumph of immortal praise
 Could rouse the languor of the lingering Boy.

Abandon'd all to soft OENONE's charms,
 He to oblivion doom'd the listless day;
Inglorious lull'd in Love's dissolving arms,
 While flutes lascivious breathed th' enfeebling lay.

To trim the ringlets of his scented hair,
 To aim, insidious, Love's bewitching glance,
To cull fresh garlands for the gaudy Fair,
 Or wanton loose in the voluptuous dance;

These were his arts; these won OENONE's love,
 Nor sought his fetter'd soul a nobler aim——
Ah why should Beauty's smile the arts approve,
 Which taint with infamy the lover's flame!

Now laid at large befide a murmuring fpring
  Melting he liften'd to the woodland fong;
And Echo liftening waved her aery wing,
  While the deep-winding dales the lays prolong.

When lo, flow-floating down the azure fkies,
  A crimfon cloud flafh'd on his ftartled fight,
Whofe fkirts gay-fparkling with unnumber'd dies
  Lanch'd the long billowy trails of flickering light.

That inftant, hufh'd was all the vocal grove,
  Hufh'd was the gale, and every ruder found;
And lays aereal warbling far above
  Rung in the ear a magic peal profound.

Near and more near the fwimming radiance roll'd,
  Along the mountains ftream'd the lingering fires;
Sublime the groves of Ida blazed with gold,
  And heaven refounded wide with louder lyres.

Upfprung

Upsprung the trump's shrill clang; and all in air
    The glories vanish'd from the dazzled eye;
And three ethereal forms, divinely fair,
    Down the steep glade were seen advancing nigh.

The flowering glade fell level where they mov'd,
    O'er-arching high the clustering roses hung,
And gales from heaven on balmy pinions rov'd,
    And hill and dale with gratulation rung.

The FIRST with slow and stately step drew near;
    Fix'd was her lofty eye, erect her mien;
Sublime in grace, in majesty severe,
    She look'd a goddess, and she mov'd a queen.

Her robe along the gale profusely stream'd,
    Light lean'd the sceptre on her bending arm;
And round her brow a starry circlet gleam'd,
    Heightening the pride of each commanding charm.

                            Milder

Milder the NEXT came on with artless grace,
  And on a javelin's quivering length reclin'd;
T' exalt her mien she bade no splendor blaze,
  Nor pomp of vesture fluctuate on the wind.

Serene, though awful, on her lofty brows,
  Celestial Wisdom shone; nor rov'd her eye,
Save where Ide's darkening cliffs majestic rose,
  Or the blue concave of th' involving sky.

Keen were her eyes, t' explore the inmost soul;
  Yet Virtue triumph'd in their beams benign;
And impious Pride oft felt their dread controul,
  When in fierce lightning flash'd the wrath divine [*].

With awe-struck wonder gazed th' adoring SWAIN;
  His kindling cheek great Virtue's power confess'd;
But soon 'twas o'er, for Virtue prompts in vain,
  When Pleasure's influence numbs the nerveless breast.

[*] This is agreeable to the Theology of Homer, who often represents Pallas as the executioner of the divine vengeance.

And now advanced the QUEEN OF MELTING JOY,
  Smiling fupreme in unrefifted charms.
Ah then, what tranfports fired the trembling BOY!
  How throb'd his fickening frame with fierce alarms!

Her fparkling eyes, all moiftening as they fwim
  Luxurious, look'd unutterable love.
Heaven's warm bloom glows along each brightening limb,
  Where fluttering bland the veil's thin mantlings rove.

Quick, blufhing as abafh'd, fhe half withdrew;
  One hand a bough of flowering myrtle wav'd,
One graceful fpread, where, fcarce conceal'd from view,
  Soft through the parting robe her bofom heav'd.

" OFFSPRING of JOVE fupreme! belov'd of heaven!
  " Attend." Thus fpoke the Emprefs of the fkies.
" For, lo, to thee, high-fated Prince, 'tis given
  " Through the bright realms of Fame fublime to rife,

" Beyond

" Beyond man's loftieft hope; if nor the wiles
   " Of PALLAS quell each bold ennobling thought;
" Nor PLEASURE lure thee, with her witching fmiles,
   " To quaff the poifon of her lufcious draught.

" When JUNO's charms the prize of beauty claim,
   " Shall ought on earth, fhall ought in heaven contend?
" Whom JUNO calls to high triumphant fame,
   " Shall he to meaner fway inglorious bend?

" Yet lingering comfortlefs in lonefome wild,
   " Where Echo fleeps mid cavern'd vales profound,
" The pride of Troy, Dominion's darling child
   " Pines, while the flow hour ftalks its fullen round.

" Hear, Thou, of heaven unconfcious! From the blaze
   " Of glory ftream'd from JOVE's eternal throne,
" Thy foul, O Mortal, caught th' infpiring rays,
   " That to a God exalt Earth's raptur'd fon.

" Hence

"Hence the bold wish, on boundless pinion born,
  " That whirls through fields of ecstacy the soul;
" The hero's eye, hence, kindling into scorn,
  " Blasts the proud menace, and defies controul.

" But, unimprov'd, heaven's noblest boons are vain.
  " No sun with plenty crowns th' uncultur'd vale;
" Where green lakes languish on the silent plain,
  " Death rides the billowings of the western gale.

" Deep in yon mountain's womb, where the dark cave
  " Howls to the torrent's everlasting roar,
" Does the rich gem its liquid radiance wave,
  " Or flames with steady ray th' imperial ore?

" Toil deck'd with glittering domes yon champaign wide,
  " And wakes yon grove-embosom'd lawns to joy;
" Th' imprison'd ore rends from the mountain's side,
  " Spangling with starry pomp the thrones of Troy.

" Fly

" Fly these soft scenes. Even now, with playful art,
" Love wreathes thy flowery ways with fatal snare;
" And nurse th' ethereal fire that warms thy heart,
 " That fire ethereal lives but by thy care.

" Lo, hovering near, on dark and dampy wing,
 " Sloth with stern patience waits the hour assign'd,
" From her chill plume the deadly dews to fling,
 " That quench heaven's beam, and freeze the chearless
  " mind.

" Vain, then, th' enlivening sound of Fame's alarms,
 " For Hope's exulting impulse prompts no more;
" Vain the false joys that lure to Pleasure's arms,
 " The throb of transport is for ever o'er.

" Ah, who shall then to Fancy's darkening eyes
 " Recal th' elysian dreams of joy and light?
" Dim through the gloom the formless visions rise,
 " Snatch'd instantaneous down the gulph of night.

" Thou, who securely lull'd in youth's warm ray,

" Hearst not the tottering wrecks o'erthrown by Time,

" Be rous'd, or perish. Ardent for its prey

" Speeds the fell hour, that desolates thy prime.

" And, midst the horrors shrin'd of midnight storm,

" The fiend Oblivion eyes thee from afar,

" Black with intolerable frowns her form,

" Beckoning th' embattled whirlwinds into war.

" Fanes, bulwarks, mountains, worlds, their tempest
" whelms;

" Yet Glory braves unmov'd th' impetuous sweep:

" Fly then, ere, hurl'd from life's delightful realms,

" Thou sink t' Oblivion's dark and boundless deep.

" Fly then, where Glory points the path sublime:

" See her crown dazzling with eternal light!

" 'Tis JUNO prompts thy daring steps to climb,

" And girds thy bounding heart with matchless might.

" Warm

" Warm in the raptures of divine defire,
   " Burft the foft chain that curbs th' afpiring mind;
" And fly, where Victory, born on wings of fire,
   " Waves her red banner to the rattling wind.

" Afcend the car. Indulge the pride of arms,
   " Where clarions roll their kindling ftrains on high,
" Where the eye maddens to the dread alarms,
   " And the long fhout tumultuous rends the fky.

" Plung'd in the uproar of the thundering field
   " I fee thy lofty arm the tempeft guide;
" Fate fcatters lightning from thy meteor-fhield,
   " And Ruin fpreads around the fanguine tide.

" Go, urge the terrors of thy headlong car
   " On proftrate Pride, and Grandeur's fpoils o'erthrown;
" While, all amaz'd, even heroes fhrink afar,
   " And hofts embattled vanifh at thy frown.

                              " When

" When Glory crowns thy godlike toils; and all
  " The triumph's lengthening pomp exalts thy foul;
" When lowly at thy feet the Mighty fall,
   " And tyrants tremble at thy ſtern controul;

" When conquering millions hail thy ſovereign might,
   " And tribes unknown dread acclamation join;
" How wilt thou ſpurn the forms of low delight!
   " For all the ecſtaſies of heaven are thine;

" For thine the joys, that fear no length of days,
   " Whoſe wide effulgence ſcorns all mortal bound:
" Fame's trump in thunder ſhall announce thy praiſe,
   " Not wrecking worlds her clarion's blaſt confound."

The Goddeſs ceas'd, not dubious of the prize;
   Elate ſhe mark'd his wild and rolling eye,
Mark'd his lip quiver, and his boſom riſe,
   And his warm cheek ſuffus'd with crimſon die.

But

But Pallas now drew near. Sublime, ferene
  In confcious dignity fhe view'd the fwain;
Then, love and pity foftening all her mien,
  Thus breathed with accent mild the folemn ftrain.

" Let thofe, whofe arts to fatal paths betray,
  " The foul with Paffion's gloom tempeftuous blind;
" And fnatch from Reafon's ken th' aufpicious ray
  " Truth darts from heaven to guide th' exploring mind.

" But wisdom loves the calm and ferious hour,
  " When heaven's pure emanation beams confefs'd;
" Rage, ecftafy, alike, difclaim her power;
  " She wooes each gentler impulfe of the breaft.

" Sincere th' unalter'd blifs her charms impart,
  " Sedate th' enlivening ardors they infpire;
" She bids no tranfient rapture thrill the heart,
  " She wakes no feverifh guft of fierce defire.

                              " Unwife,

" Unwife, who, toffing on the watery way,

 " All to the ftorm th' unfetter'd fail devolve;

" Man more unwife refigns the mental fway,

 " Born headlong on by Paffion's keen refolve.

" While ftorms remote but murmur on thine ear,

 " Nor waves in ruinous uproar round thee roll,

" Yet yet a moment check thy prone career,

 " And curb the keen refolve that prompts thy foul.

" Explore thy heart, that, rous'd by Glory's name,

 " Pants all enraptur'd with the mighty charm;—

" And does Ambition quench each milder flame?

 " And is it Conqueft, that alone can warm?

" T' indulge fell Rapine's defolating luft,

 " To drench the balmy lawn in fteaming gore,

" To fpurn the hero's cold and filent duft;—

 " Are thefe thy joys? not throbs thy heart for more?

" Pleas'd

" Pleas'd canst thou listen to the patriot's groan,
  " And the wild wail of Innocence forlorn?
" And hear th' abandon'd maid's last frantic moan,
  " Her Love for ever from her bosom torn?

" Nor wilt thou shrink, when Virtue's fainting breath
  " Pours the dread curse of vengeance on thy head?
" Nor when the pale ghost bursts the cave of death,
  " To glare distraction on thy midnight bed?

" Was it for this, though born to regal power,
  " Kind heaven to thee did nobler gifts consign;
" Bade Fancy's influence gild thy natal hour,
  " And bade Philanthropy's applause be thine?

" Theirs be the dreadful glory to destroy,
  " And theirs the pride of pomp, and praise suborn'd,
" Whose eye ne'er lighten'd at the smile of Joy,
  " Whose cheek the tear of Pity ne'er adorn'd;

" Whose

" Whose soul, each finer sense instinctive quell'd,
  " The Lyre's mellifluous ravishment defies,
" Nor marks where Beauty roves the flowering field,
  " Or Grandeur's pinion sweeps th' unbounded skies.

" Hail to sweet Fancy's unexpressive charm!
  " Hail to the pure delights of social love!
" Hail, pleasures mild, that fire not while ye warm,
  " Nor rack th' exulting frame, but gently move!

" But Fancy soothes no more, if stern Remorse
  " With iron grasp the tortur'd bosom wring:
" Ah then, even Fancy speeds the venom's course,
  " Even Fancy points with rage the maddening sting.

" Her wrath a thousand gnashing fiends attend,
  " And roll the snakes, and toss the brands of hell:
" The beam of Beauty blasts, dark heavens impend
  " Tottering, and Music thrills with startling yell.

" What

" What then avails, that, with exhaustless store,

" Obsequious Luxury loads thy glittering shrine?

" What then avails, that prostrate slaves adore,

" And Fame proclaims thee matchless and divine?

" What, though bland Flattery all her arts apply?---

" Will these avail to calm th' infuriate brain?

" Or will the roaring surge, when heav'd on high,

" Headlong hang, hush'd to hear the piping swain?

" In health how fair, how ghastly in decay

" Man's lofty form! how heavenly fair the mind

" Sublimed by Virtue's sweet enlivening sway!

" But ah! to Guilt's outrageous rule resign'd,

" How hideous and forlorn! where ruthless Care

" With cankering tooth corrodes the seeds of life;

" And, deaf with Passion's storms, where pines Despair;

" And howling furies rouse th' eternal strife.

" O, by thy hopes of joy, that reftlefs glow,

" Pledges of heaven! be taught by Wifdom's lore;

" With anxious hafte each doubtful path forego,

" And life's wild ways with cautious fear explore.

" Straight be thy courfe; nor tempt the maze that leads

" Where fell Remorfe his fhapelefs ftrength conceals:

" And oft Ambition's dizzy cliff he treads,

" And flumbers oft in Pleafure's flowery vales.

" Nor linger unrefolv'd; heaven prompts the choice,

" Save when prefumption fhuts the ear of Pride:

" With grateful awe attend to Nature's voice,

" The voice of Nature heaven ordain'd thy guide.

" Warn'd by her voice the arduous path purfue,

" That leads to Virtue's fane a fcanty band.

" What, though no gaudy fcenes decoy their view,

" Nor clouds of fragrance roll along the land?

" What,

" What, though rude mountains heave the flinty way?
" Yet there the foul drinks light and life divine;
" And pure aereal gales of gladnefs play,
" Brace every nerve, and every fenfe refine.

" Go, Prince, be virtuous, and be bleft. The throne
" Rears not its ftate to fwell the couch of Luft;
" Nor dignify Corruption's daring fon,
" T' o'erwhelm his humbler brethren of the duft;.

" But yield an ampler fcene to Bounty's eye;
" An ampler range to Mercy's ear expand;
" And, midft admiring nations, fet on high
" Virtue's fair model framed by Wifdom's hand.

" Go then; the voice of Woe demands thine aid;
" Pride's licens'd outrage claims thy flumbering ire;
" Pale Genius roams the chill neglected fhade,
" And torpid Avarice mocks his tunelefs lyre.

" Even

" Even Nature pines, by vileſt chains oppreſs'd;
 " Th' aſtoniſh'd kingdoms crouch to Faſhion's nod.
" O ye pure inmates of the gentle breaſt,
 " Truth, Freedom, Love, O where is your abode?

" O yet once more ſhall Peace from heaven return,
 " And young Simplicity with mortals dwell!
" Nor Innocence th' auguſt pavilion ſcorn,
 " Nor meek Contentment fly the humble cell!

" Wilt thou, my Prince, the beauteous train implore
 " Midſt earth's forſaken ſcenes once more to bide?
" Then Solitude ſhall ſing in every bower,
 " And Love with garlands wreathe the domes of Pride.

" The tears bright-ſtarting in th' impaſſion'd eyes
 " Of ſilent Gratitude; the ſmiling gaze
" Of Gratulation, faultering, while he tries
 " With voice of rapturous joy to tell thy praiſe;

" Th'

" Th' ethereal glow, that ſtimulates thy frame,
" When all th' according powers harmonious move,
" And wake to energy each ſocial aim,
" Attuned ſpontaneous to the will of Jove:

" Be theſe, O Man, the triumphs of thy ſoul;
" And all the Conqueror's dazzling glories ſlight,
" That, meteor-like, o'er trembling nations roll,
" To ſink at once in deep and dreadful night.

" Like thine, yon Orb's ſtupendous glories burn
" With genial beam; nor, at th' approach of even,
" In ſhades of horror leave the world to mourn,
" But gild with lingering light th' empurpled heaven."

Thus while She ſpoke, her eye ſedately meek
  Look'd the pure fervor of maternal love;
No rival Zeal intemperate fluſh'd her cheek ---
  Can Beauty's boaſt the ſoul of Wiſdom move?

Worth's

Worth's noble pride can Envy's leer appal,
 Or staring Folly's vain applauses soothe?
Can jealous fear Truth's dauntless heart enthral?
 Suspicion lurks not in the heart of Truth.

And now the SHEPHERD rais'd his pensive head.
 Yet unresolv'd and fearful rov'd his eyes,
Nor dared the glances of the AWEFUL MAID;
 For young unpractis'd Guilt distrusts the guise

Of shameless arrogance. His wavering breast,
 Though warm'd by Wisdom, own'd no constant fire;
While lawless fancy roam'd afar, unblest,
 Save in the oblivious lap of soft desire.

When thus the QUEEN of soul-dissolving smiles:
 " LET gentler fates my darling Prince attend.
" Joyless and cruel are the warrior's spoils,
 " Dreary the path stern Virtue's sons ascend.

" Of mortal joy full narrow is the space,
  " And the dread verge still gains upon the sight;
" While, far beyond his sphere, man's empty gaze
  " Scans the faint dream of unapproach'd delight;

" Till every sprightly hour, and blooming scene
  " Of life's gay morn, unheeded, glides away,
" Clouds fraught with tempest mount the blue serene,
  " And storm and ruin close the troublous day.

" Thou still exult to hail the present joy;
  " Thine be the boon that comes unearn'd by toil;
" No froward vain desire thy bliss annoy,
  " No flattering hope thy longing hours beguile!

" Ah! why should man pursue the charms of Fame,
  " For ever luring, yet for ever coy?
" Light as the gaudy rainbow's pillar'd gleam,
  " That melts elusive from the wondering boy!

E " What,

" What, though her throne irradiate many a clime,
 " If hung loose-tottering o'er th' unfathom'd tomb?
" What, though her mighty clarion, rear'd sublime,
 " Display th' imperial wreathe, and glittering plume?

" Can glittering plume, or can th' imperial wreathe
 " Redeem, from unrelenting Fate, the brave?
" What note of triumph can her clarion breathe,
 " T' alarm th' eternal midnight of the grave?

" That night draws on; nor will the vacant hour
 " Of expectation linger as it flies,
" Nor fate one moment unenjoy'd restore;
 " Each moment's flight how precious to the wise!

" O shun th' annoyance of the bustling throng,
 " That haunt with zealous turbulence the Great.
" There coward Office boasts th' unpunish'd wrong,
 " And sneaks secure in insolence of state:

"O'er

" O'er fancy'd injury Sufpicion pines,

" And in grim filence gnaws the feftering wound;

" Deceit the rage-embitter'd fmile refines,

" And Cenfure fpreads the viperous hifs around.

" Hope not, fond Prince, though Wifdom guard thy
" throne,

" Though Truth and Bounty prompt each generous aim,

" Though thine the palm of peace, the victor's crown,

" The mufe's rapture, and the patriot's flame;

" Hope not, though all that captivates the wife,

" All that endears the good exalt thy praife,

" Hope not to tafte repofe; for Envy's eyes

" At faireft worth ftill point their deadly rays.

" Envy, ftern tyrant of the flinty heart,

" Can ought of virtue, truth, or beauty charm?

" Can foft Compaffion thrill with pleafing fmart,

" Repentance melt, or Gratitude difarm?

" Ah

" Ah no.   Where Winter Scythia's wafte enchains,
   " And monftrous fhapes growl to the ruthlefs ftorm,
" Not Phæbus' fmile can chear the dreadful plains,
   " Or foil accurs'd with balmy life inform.

" Then, Envy, then is thy triumphant hour,
   " When mourns Benevolence his baffled fcheme;
" When Infult mocks the clemency of Power,
   " And loud Diffention's livid firebrands gleam;

" When fquint-eyed Slander plies th' unhallow'd tongue,
   " From poifon'd maw when Treafon weaves his line,
" And mufe apoftate (infamy to fong!)
   " Grovels, low-muttering at Sedition's fhrine.

" Let not my Prince forego the tranquil fhade,
   " The whifpering grove, the fountain, and the plain:
" Power, with the oppreffive weight of pomp array'd,
   " Pants for fimplicity and eafe --- in vain.

                                           " The

" The yell of frantic Mirth may ſtun his ear;
  " But frantic Mirth ſoon leaves the heart forlorn;
" And PLEASURE flies that high tempeſtuous ſphere,
  " Far different ſcenes her lucid paths adorn.

" She loves to wander on th' untrodden lawn,
  " Or the green boſom of reclining hill,
" Sooth'd by the careleſs warbler of the dawn,
  " Or the lone plaint of ever-murmuring rill.

" Or, from the mountain-glade's aëreal brow,
  " While to her ſong a thouſand echoes call,
" Marks the wild woodland wave remote below,
  " Where ſhepherds pipe unſeen, and waters fall.

" Her influence oft the feſtive hamlet proves,
  " Where the high carol chears th' exulting ring;
" And oft ſhe roams the maze of wildering groves,
  " Liſtening the unnumber'd melodies of ſpring:

" Or

" Or to the long and lonely shore retires;
 " What time, loose-glimmering to the lunar beam,
" Faint heaves the slumberous wave, and starry fires
 " Gild the blue deep with many a lengthening gleam:

" Then, to the balmy bower of rapture born,
 " While strings, self-warbling, breathe elysian rest,
" Melts in delicious vision, till the Morn
 " Spangle with twinkling dew the flowery waste.

" The frolic Moments, purple-pinion'd, dance
 " Around, and scatter roses as they play;
" And the blithe Graces, hand in hand, advance,
 " Where, with her lov'd Compeers, she deigns to stray:

" Mild Solitude, in veil of russet die,
 " Her sylvan spear with moss-grown ivy bound;
" And Indolence, with sweetly-languid eye,
 " And zoneless robe that trails along the ground.

" But

" But chiefly Love ---- O Thou, whose gentle mind
   " Each soft indulgence Nature framed to share;
" Pomp, wealth, renown, dominion, all resign'd,
   " O haste to Pleasure's bower; for Love is there.

" Love, the desire of Gods! the feast of heaven!
   " Yet to earth's favour'd offspring not deny'd!
" Ah, let not thankless man the blessing given
   " Enslave to fame, or sacrifice to pride.

" Nor I from Virtue's call decoy thine ear;
   " Friendly to Pleasure are her sacred laws.
" Let Temperance' smile the cup of gladness chear,
   " That cup is death, if he with-hold applause.

" Far from thy haunt be Envy's baneful sway,
   " And Hate that works the harrass'd soul to storm;
" But woo Content to breathe her soothing lay,
   " And charm from Fancy's view each angry form.

                                               " No

" No favage joy th' harmonious hours profane!

   " Whom love refines can barbarous tumult pleafe?

" Shall rage of blood pollute the fylvan reign?

   " Shall Leifure wanton in the fpoils of Peace?

" Free let the feathery race indulge the fong,

   " Inhale the liberal beam, and melt in love;

" Free let the fleet hind bound her hills along,

   " And in pure ftreams the watery nations rove.

" To joy in Nature's univerfal fmile,

   " Well fuits, O Man, thy pleafurable fphere;

" But why fhould Virtue doom thy years to toil!

   " Ah, why fhould Virtue's law be deem'd fevere!

" What meed, Beneficence, thy care repays?

   " What, Sympathy, thy ftill-returning pang?

" And why his generous arm fhould Juftice raife,

   " To dare the vengeance of a tyrant's fang?

                                              " From

" From thankless Spite no bounty can secure;
　" Or froward wish of Discontent fulfil,
" That knows not to regret thy bounded power,
　" But blames with keen reproach thy partial will.

" To check th' impetuous all-involving tide
　" Of human woes, how impotent thy strife!
" High o'er thy mounds devouring surges ride,
　" Nor reck thy baffled toils, or lavish'd life.

" The bower of bliss, the smile of love be thine,
　" Unlabour'd ease, and leisure's careless dream.
" Such be their joys, who bend at Venus' shrine,
　" And own her charms beyond compare supreme!"

Warm'd, as she spoke, all panting with delight,
　Her kindling beauties breathed triumphant bloom,
And Cupids flutter'd round in circlets bright,
　And Flora pour'd from all her stores perfume.

F　　　　　　　　" Thine

"Thine be the prize;" exclaim'd th' enraptur'd Youth,
  "Queen of unrival'd charms, and matchlefs joy!"—
O blind to fate, felicity, and truth!——
  But fuch are they, whom Pleafure's fnares decoy.

The fun was funk, the vifion was no more.
  Night downward rufh'd tempeftuous, at the frown
Of Jove's awaken'd wrath; deep thunders roar,
  The forefts howl afar, and mountains groan.

Fierce-whirling meteors glare athwart the plain;
  With horror's fcream the Ilian towers refound;
Raves the hoarfe ftorm along the bellowing main,
  And the ftrong earthquake rends the fhuddering ground.

THE END.

VERSES.

Occasioned by the DEATH of

The Rev.^d Mr CHARLES CHURCHILL.

VERSES

Occasioned by the Death of

The Rev^d. Mr CHARLES CHURCHILL.

Written by a Native of BRITAIN.
---

*Difficile est Satiram non scribere: Nam quis iniquæ
Tam patiens urbis, tam ferreus, ut teneat se!*
                                JUVENAL.

LONDON:
M.DCC.LXV.

On the Death of

The Rev^d. Mr CHARLES CHURCHILL.

CHURCHILL begone! with thee may discord's fire,
That hatch'd thy salamander-fame, expire!
Fame, dirty idol of the brainless crowd,
What half-made mooncalf can mistake for good!
Since shar'd by knaves of high and low degree,
Cromwel and Catiline, Guido Fawkes and thee.

By nature uninspir'd, untaught by art,
With not one thought that breathes the feeling heart,
With not one offering vow'd to Virtue's shrine,
With not one pure unprostituted line;

The

The hireling slave of faction and of spite,

His country's nuisance, and a Wilkes' delight;

Alike debauch'd in body, soul, and lays;—

—For pension'd censure, and for pension'd praise;

For ribaldry, for libels, lewdness, lies,

For blasphemy of all the good and wise;

Coarse virulence in coarser dogrel writ,

Which bawling blackguards spell'd, and took for wit;

For conscience, honour, slighted, spurn'd, o'erthrown;—

Lo, Churchill shines the minion of renown!

Is this the land that boasts a MILTON's fire,

And magic SPENSER's wildly-warbling lyre?

The land that owns th' omnipotence of song,

When SHAKESPEAR whirls the throbbing heart along?

The

The land, where POPE, with energy divine,

In one strong blaze bade wit and fancy shine;

Whose verse, by truth, in virtue's triumph born,

Gave knaves to infamy, and fools to scorn;

Yet pure in manners, and in thought refin'd,

Whose life and lays adorn'd and bless'd mankind?

Is this the land, where GRAY's unlabour'd art

Soothes, melts, alarms, and ravishes the heart;

While the lone wanderer's sweet complainings flow

In simple majesty of manly woe;

Or while, sublime, on eagle pinion driven,

He soars Pindaric heights, and sails the waste of heaven?

Is this the land o'er SHENSTONE's recent urn,

Where all the loves and gentler graces mourn?

And

And where, t' adorn the hoary * Bard of night,
The muses and the virtues all unite?
Is this the land, where AKENSIDE displays
The bold, yet temp'rate flame of antient days?
Like the rapt † Sage in genius, as in theme,
Whose hallow'd strain renown'd Ilissus' stream:
Or him, ‡ th' indignant Bard, whose patriot ire,
Sublime in vengeance, smote the dreadful lyre;
For truth, for liberty, for virtue warm,
Whose mighty song unnerv'd a tyrant's arm,
Hush'd the rude roar of discord, rage, and lust,
And spurn'd licentious demagogues to dust.

Is this the Queen of realms! the glorious isle,
BRITANNIA, bless'd in heav'n's indulgent smile!
Guardian of truth, and patroness of art,
Nurse of th' undaunted soul, and generous heart!

Where

* Young. † Plato. ‡ Alcæus. See Akenside's ode on lyric poetry.

Where, from a base degenerate world exil'd,
Freedom exults to roam the careless wild;
Where taste to science every charm supplies,
And genius soars unbounded to the skies!

 And shall a Churchill's most polluted name
Stain her bright tablet of untainted fame?
Shall his disgraceful name with their's be join'd,
Who wish'd and wrought the welfare of their kind?
His name accurs'd, who leagued with Wilkes and hell,
Labour'd to rouse, with rude and murderous yell,
Discord the fiend, to toss rebellion's brand,
In rage and ruin whelm a guiltless land;
To frustrate virtue's wisdom's noblest plan,
And triumph in the miseries of man.

Driveling and dull when crawls the reptile-
 muse,

Swoln from the sty, and rankling from the stews,

With poison, spleen, and pestilence replete,

Gorg'd with the dust she lick'd from treason's feet,

Who once, like Satan, rais'd to heaven her sight,

But turn'd abhorrent from the hated light;—

O'er such a muse shall wreathes of glory bloom?

No—Shame and execration be her doom.

Hard-fated Churchill! Could not dullness save

Thy soul from sin, from infamy thy grave!

Blackmore and Quarles, those blockheads of
 renown,

Lavish'd their ink, but never harm'd the town;

Though this, thy rival in discordant song,

Harass'd the ear, and cramp'd the labouring
 tongue;

And

And that, like thee, taught staggering prose to stand,
And limp on stilts of ryhme around the land;
Harmless they doz'd a scribbling life away,
And yawning nations own'd th' innoxious lay.
But from thy graceless, rude, and beastly brain,
What fury breath'd th' incendiary strain!
Did hate to vice exasperate thy style?
No—Churchill match'd the vilest of the vile.
Yet blazon'd was his verse with Virtue's name—
Thus prudes look down to hide their want of shame;
Thus hypocrites to truth, and fools to sense,
And fops to taste, have sometimes made pretence;
Thus thieves and gamesters swear by honour's laws;
Thus pension-hunters bawl *their country's cause;*

Thus Teague for moderation furious rav'd,
And own'd his foul to liberty enflav'd.

Nor yet, tho' thoufand Cits admire thy rage,
Tho' lefs of fool than felon marks thy page;
Nor yet, tho' here and there one lonely fpark
Of wit half-brighten's thro' th' involving dark,
To fhow the gloom more hideous for the foil,
But not repay the drudging reader's toil,
(For who for one poor pearl of clouded ray
Thro' Alpine dunghills delves his defperate way?)
Did genius to thy verfe fuch bane impart?
No. 'Twas the demon of thy venom'd heart,
(Thy heart with rancour's quinteffence endow'd)
And the blind zeal of a misjudging crowd.
Thus from rank foil a poifon'd mufhrom fprung,
Nurfeling obfcene of mildew and of dung;

By heaven defigned on its own native fpot

Harmlefs t' enlarge its bloated bulk, and rot:

But Gluttony the abortive nuifance faw;

It rous'd his ravenous undifcerning maw;

Gulp'd down the taftelefs throat, the mefs abhor'd,

Shot fiery influence round the maddening board.

O! had thy verfe been impotent, as dull,

Nor fpoke thy rage of heart, but weight of fcull:

Had mobs diftinguifh'd, while they howl'd thy fame,

The icicle from the pure diamond's flame,

From fancy's foul thy grofs imbruted fenfe,

From dauntlefs truth thy fhamelefs infolence,

From elegance, confufion's monftrous mafs,

And from the lyon's fpoils the fculking afs,

From

From rapture's strain the drawling dogrel line,

From warbling seraphim the gruntling swine :—

With gluttons, dunces, rakes, thy name had slept,

Nor o'er her sullied fame Britannia wept;

Nor had the muse, with honest zeal possess'd,

T' avenge her country by thy name disgrac'd,

Rais'd this bold strain for virtue, truth, mankind;

And thy fell shade to infamy resign'd.

When frailty leads astray the soul sincere,

Let mercy shed the soft and manly tear.

When to the grave descends the sensual sot,

Unnam'd, unnotic'd let his carrion rot.

When paltry rogues, by stealth, deceit, or force,

Hazard their necks, ambitious of your purse;

For these the hangman wreathes his trusty gin,

And let the gallows expiate their sin.

But

But when a ruffian, whose portentous crimes,
Like plagues and earthquakes, terrify the times,
Triumphs thro' life, from legal judgment free,
For hell may hatch what law could ne'er foresee:
Sacred from vengeance shall his memory rest?—
Judas, tho' dead, tho' damn'd, we still detest.

THE END.

To Mr Alexander Ross at Lochlee

To the Printer of the Aberdeen Journal.

SIR,

I have read the Fortunate Shepherdefs, and other Poems in Broad Scotch, juft publifhed at Aberdeen, by Mr Alexr Rofs of Lochlee. This writer has given us the provincial dialects of Angus, Mearns, and Aberdeenfhire, in great perfection; and I am convinced his work will be highly amufing to all who relifh that fort of compofition. A nice critic might perhaps take exception at his plot, at the prolixity of fome of his fpeeches, and at the impropriety of fome particular incidents and fentiments: but Mr Rofs, in his preface, hath made fo modeft an acknowledgment of thefe, and the other faults which he thinks may be found in the performance, that it is impoffible for a good-natured reader not to excufe them. Many genuine ftrokes of nature and paffion, and many beautiful touches of picturefque defcription, are to be feen in this work. There is even an attempt at character, which in one or two inftances is by no means unfuccefsful.—In his Songs there is an eafy turn of humour and verfification: fome of them have long been known to the common people of this country, who fing them with much fatisfaction and goodhumour. I beg leave to tranfmit to this facetious author, by the channel of your paper, the following lines, which may pleafe fome of your readers, and cannot, I think, offend any: and am, Sir,

Your humble Servant,

June 1, 1768. OLIVER OLDSTILE.

To Mr. ALEXANDER ROSS at Lochlee,
    Author of the Fortunate Shepherdess, and
    other Poems, in the Broad Scotch Dialect.

O Ross, thou wale of hearty cocks,
    Sae crouse and canty wi' thy jokes!
Thy hamely auldwarld muse provokes
        Me, for a while,
To ape our guid plain countra' folks
        In verse and stile.

Sure never carle was haff sae gabby,
E're since the winsome days of Habby.
O mayst thou ne'er gang clung or shabby,
        Nor miss thy snaker!
Or I'll ca' Fortune, Nasty Drabby,
        And say, Pox take her.

O may the roupe ne'er roust thy weason!
May thirst thy thrapple never gizzen!
But bottled ale, in mony a dozen,
        Ay lade thy gantry!
And fowth o' vivers, a' in season,
        Plenish thy pantry!

Lang may thy stevin fill wi' glee
The glens and mountains of Lochlee,
Which were right gowsty but for thee,
        Whase sangs enamour
Ilk lass, and teach wi' melody
        The rocks to yamour.

Ye shak your head; bat, o' my fegs,
Ye've set auld SCOTA (*a*) on her legs.
Lang had she lyen, wi' beffs and flegs
        Bumbaz'd and dizzie,
Her fiddle wanted strings and pegs:
        Waes me! poor hizzie!

Since Allan's death, naebody car'd
For anes to speer how Scota far'd;
Nor plack nor thristled turner war'd,
        To quench her drouth;

(*a*) The Name Mr Ross gives to his Muse.

For, frae the cottar to the laird,
           We a' rin South.
The Southland chiels indeed hae mettle,
And brawly at a fang can ettle;
Yet we right couthily might settle
           O' this side Forth.
The devil pay them wi' a pettle,
           That slight the North.
Our countra' leed is far frae barren,
It's even right pithy and aulfarren,
Ourfells are neiper-like, I warran,
           For sense and smergh,
In kittle times, whan faes are yarring,
           We're no thought ergh.
O bonny are our greensward hows,
Where through the birks the burny rows,
And the bee bums, and the ox lows,
           And saft winds rusle,
And shepherd-lads on sunny knows,
           Blaw the blythe fusle.
It's true, we norlans manna fa'
To eat sae nice, or gang sae bra',
As they that come frae far awa';
           Yet sma's our skaith:
We've peace (and that's well worth it a')
           And meat and claith.
Our fine newfangle sparks, I grant ye,
Gie poor auld Scotland mony a taunty;
They're grown sae ugertfu' and vaunty,
           And capernoited,
They guide her like a canker'd aunty,
           That's deaf and doited.
Sae comes of Ignorance, I trow,
It's this that crooks their ill-fa'rd mou'
Wi' jokes sae courfe, they gar fouk spue
           For downright skonner.
For Scotland wants na sons enew
           To do her honour.

I here might gie a screed of names,
Dawties of Heliconian Dames!
The foremost place Gawin Douglas (*b*) claims,
    That canty priest.
And wha can match the fifth King James (*c*)
    For sang or jest?
Montgomery (*d*) grave, and Ramsay gay,
Dunbar (*e*), Scot (*f*), Hawthornden, and mae
Than I can tell, for o' my fae,
    I maun brak aff;
'Twould tak a live-lang summer-day
    To name the haff.
The saucy chiels——I think they ca' them
Criticks——the muckle sorrow claw them,
(For mense nor manners ne'er could awe them
    Frae their presumption)
They need na try thy jokes to fathom,
    They want rumgumption.
But ilka Mearns and Angus bairn
Thy tales and sangs by heart shall learn;
And chiels shall come frae yont the Cairn-
    amounth, right vousty,
L...s will be so kind as share in
    Their pint at Drousty (*g*).

(*b*) Bishop of Dunkeld, the celebrated translator of Virgil's Eneid. He died 1522.

(*c*) The Author of Christ's Kirk on the Green, The Gaberlunzie-man, &c.

(*d*) He wrote the Cherry and the Slae.

(*e*) Author of the Thistle and Rose.

(*f*) Author of the Vision, a Poem remarkable for pathos and elegance of description.

(*g*) An Alehouse in Lochlee.

THE MINSTREL,

IN TWO BOOKS:

WITH

SOME OTHER POEMS.

BY

JAMES BEATTIE, LL.D.

A NEW EDITION.

LONDON:

PRINTED FOR CHARLES DILLY, IN THE POULTRY;
AND W. CREECH, IN EDINBURGH.
MDCCLXXXIV.

ADVERTISEMENT.

January, 1777.

HAVING lately seen in print some poems ascribed to me, which I never wrote, and some of my own inaccurately copied, I thought it would not be improper to publish, in this little volume, all the verses of which I am willing to be considered as the author. Many others I did indeed write in the early part of my life; but they were in general so incorrect, that I would not rescue them from oblivion, even if a wish could do it.

Some of the few now offered to the Public would perhaps have been suppressed, if in making this collection I had implicitly followed my own judgment. But in so small a matter who would refuse to submit his opinion to that of a friend?

It is of no consequence to the reader to know the date of any of these little poems.

ADVERTISEMENT.

But some private reasons determine the author to add, that most of them were written many years ago, and that the greater part of the Minstrel, which is his latest attempt in this way, was composed in the year one thousand seven hundred and sixty-eight.

THE
CONTENTS.

THE Minstrel. Book I. — Page 1
———— Book II. — 33
Retirement — — 65
Elegy — — — 69
Ode to Hope — — — 73
Pygmæo-gerano-machia: The Battle of the Pygmies and Cranes — 79
The Hares: A Fable — — 89
Epitaph: Being part of an inscription for a monument, to be erected by a gentleman, to the memory of his Lady — 99
Ode on Lord H**'s birth-day — 100
The Hermit — — — 105

THE MINSTREL;

OR,

THE PROGRESS OF GENIUS.

A POEM,

IN TWO BOOKS.

THE EIGHTH EDITION, CORRECTED.

PREFACE

TO THE

MINSTREL.

THE design was, to trace the progress of a Poetical Genius, born in a rude age, from the first dawning of fancy and reason, till that period at which he may be supposed capable of appearing in the world as A Minstrel, that is, as an itinerant Poet and Musician;—a character which, according to the notions of our forefathers, was not only respectable, but sacred.

I have endeavoured to imitate Spenser in the measure of his verse, and in the harmony, simplicity, and variety, of his composition. Antique expressions I have avoided; admitting, however, some old words, where they seemed to suit the subject: but I hope none will be found that are now obsolete, or in any degree not intelligible to a reader of English poetry.

To those, who may be disposed to ask, what could induce me to write in so difficult a measure, I can only answer, that it pleases my ear, and seems, from its Gothick structure and original, to bear some relation to the subject and spirit of the Poem. It admits both simplicity and magnificence of sound and of language, beyond any other stanza that I am acquainted with. It allows the sententiousness of the couplet, as well as the more complex modulation of blank verse. What some criticks have remarked, of its uniformity growing at last tiresome to the ear, will be found to hold true, only when the poetry is faulty in other respects.

TO

Mrs. MONTAGU,

THESE LITTLE POEMS,

NOW REVISED AND CORRECTED
FOR THE LAST TIME,

ARE,

WITH EVERY SENTIMENT OF
ESTEEM AND GRATITUDE,

MOST RESPECTFULLY INSCRIBED

BY

THE AUTHOR.

THE MINSTREL;

OR, THE PROGRESS OF GENIUS.

THE FIRST BOOK.

I.

AH! who can tell how hard it is to climb
   The steep where Fame's proud temple shines afar;
Ah! who can tell how many a soul sublime
Has felt the influence of malignant star,
And waged with fortune an eternal war;
Check'd by the scoff of Pride, by Envy's frown,
And Poverty's unconquerable bar,
In life's low vale remote has pined alone,
Then dropt into the grave, unpitied and unknown!

II.

And yet, the languor of inglorious days
Not equally oppreffive is to all.
Him, who ne'er liften'd to the voice of praife,
The filence of neglect can ne'er appal.
There are, who, deaf to mad ambition's call,
Would fhrink to hear th' obftreperous trump of
    Fame;
Supremely bleft, if to their portion fall
    Health, competence, and peace. Nor higher aim
Had HE, whofe fimple tale thefe artlefs lines proclaim.

III.

The rolls of fame I will not now explore;
Nor need I here defcribe in learned lay,
How forth THE MINSTREL fared in days of yore,
Right glad of heart, though homely in array;
His waving locks and beard all hoary grey:
While from his bending fhoulder, decent hung
His harp, the fole companion of his way,
Which to the whiftling wind refponfive rung:
And ever as he went fome merry lay he fung.

IV.

Fret not thyself, thou glittering child of pride,
That a poor Villager inspires my strain;
With thee let Pageantry and Power abide:
The gentle Muses haunt the sylvan reign;
Where through wild groves at eve the lonely swain
Enraptured roams, to gaze on Nature's charms.
They hate the sensual, and scorn the vain,
The parasite their influence never warms,
Nor him whose sordid soul the love of gold alarms.

V.

Though richest hues the peacock's plumes adorn,
Yet horror screams from his discordant throat.
Rise, sons of harmony! and hail the morn,
While warbling larks on russet pinions float:
Or seek at noon the woodland scene remote,
Where the grey linnets carol from the hill.
O let them ne'er, with artificial note,
To please a tyrant, strain the little bill,
But sing what heaven inspires, and wander where they will.

VI.

Liberal, not lavish, is kind Nature's hand;
Nor was perfection made for man below.
Yet all her schemes with nicest art are plann'd,
Good counteracting ill, and gladness wo.
With gold and gems if Chilian mountains glow;
If bleak and barren Scotia's hills arise;
There plague and poison, lust and rapine grow;
Here peaceful are the vales, and pure the skies,
And freedom fires the soul, and sparkles in the eyes.

VII.

Then grieve not, thou, to whom th' indulgent
    Muse
Vouchsafes a portion of celestial fire;
Nor blame the partial Fates, if they refuse
Th' imperial banquet, and the rich attire.
Know thine own worth, and reverence the lyre.
Wilt thou debase the heart which God refined?
No; let thy heaven-taught soul to heaven aspire,
  To fancy, freedom, harmony, resign'd;
Ambition's groveling crew for ever left behind.

VIII.

Canst thou forego the pure ethereal soul
In each fine sense so exquisitely keen,
On the dull couch of Luxury to loll,
Stung with disease, and stupefied with spleen;
Fain to implore the aid of Flattery's screen,
Even from thyself thy loathsome heart to hide,
(The mansion then no more of joy serene),
Where fear, distrust, malevolence, abide,
And impotent desire, and disappointed pride?

IX.

O how canst thou renounce the boundless store
Of charms which Nature to her votary yields!
The warbling woodland, the resounding shore,
The pomp of groves, and garniture of fields;
All that the genial ray of morning gilds,
And all that echoes to the song of even,
All that the mountain's sheltering bosom shields,
And all the dread magnificence of heaven,
O how canst thou renounce, and hope to be forgiven!

X.

These charms shall work thy soul's eternal health,
And love, and gentleness, and joy, impart.
But these thou must renounce, if lust of wealth
E'er win its way to thy corrupted heart:
For, ah! it poisons like a scorpion's dart;
Prompting th' ungenerous wish, the selfish scheme,
The stern resolve unmoved by pity's smart,
The troublous day, and long distressful dream.
Return, my roving Muse, resume thy purposed theme.

XI.

There lived in Gothick days, as legends tell,
A shepherd-swain, a man of low degree;
Whose fires, perchance, in Fairyland might dwell,
Sicilian groves, or vales of Arcady;
But he, I ween, was of the north countrie *:
A nation famed for song, and beauty's charms;
Zealous, yet modest; innocent, though free;
Patient of toil; serene amidst alarms;
Inflexible in faith; invincible in arms.

---

* There is hardly an ancient ballad, or romance, wherein a Minstrel or Harper appears, but he is characterised, by way of eminence, to have been " OF THE NORTH COUNTRIE." It is

XII.

The shepherd-swain of whom I mention made,
On Scotia's mountains fed his little flock;
The sickle, scythe, or plough, he never sway'd;
An honest heart was almost all his stock;
His drink the living water from the rock;
The milky dams supplied his board, and lent
Their kindly fleece to baffle winter's shock;
And he, though oft with dust and sweat besprent,
Did guide and guard their wanderings, wheresoe'er
    they went.

XIII.

From labour health, from health contentment
    springs.
Contentment opes the source of every joy.
He envied not, he never thought of, kings;
Nor from those appetites sustain'd annoy,
That chance may frustrate, or indulgence cloy:
Nor Fate his calm and humble hopes beguiled;
He mourn'd no recreant friend, nor mistress coy,
For on his vows the blameless Phœbe smiled,
And her alone he loved, and loved her from a child.

---

probable, that under this appellation were formerly comprehended all the provinces to the north of the Trent.
        See Percy's Essay on the English Minstrels.

XIV.

No jealoufy their dawn of love o'ercaft,
Nor blafted were their wedded days with ftrife;
Each feafon look'd delightful, as it paft,
To the fond hufband, and the faithful wife.
Beyond the lowly vale of fhepherd life
They never roam'd; fecure beneath the ftorm
Which in ambition's lofty land is rife,
Where peace and love are canker'd by the worm
Of pride, each bud of joy induftrious to deform.

XV.

The wight, whofe tale thefe artlefs lines unfold,
Was all the offspring of this humble pair.
His birth no oracle or feer foretold:
No prodigy appear'd in earth or air,
Nor aught that might a ftrange event declare.
You guefs each circumftance of Edwin's birth;
The parent's tranfport, and the parent's care;
The goffip's prayer for wealth, and wit, and worth;
And one long fummer-day of indolence and mirth.

XVI.

And yet poor Edwin was no vulgar boy;
Deep thought oft seem'd to fix his infant eye.
Dainties he heeded not, nor gaude, nor toy,
Save one short pipe of rudest minstrelsy.
Silent when glad; affectionate, though shy;
And now his look was most demurely sad;
And now he laugh'd aloud, yet none knew why.
The neighbours stared and sigh'd, yet bless'd the lad:
Some deem'd him wondrous wise, and some believed him mad.

XVII.

But why should I his childish feats display?
Concourse, and noise, and toil, he ever fled;
Nor cared to mingle in the clamorous fray
Of squabbling imps; but to the forest sped;
Or roam'd at large the lonely mountain's head;
Or, where the maze of some bewilder'd stream
To deep untrodden groves his footsteps led,
There would he wander wild, till Phœbus' beam,
Shot from the western cliff, released the weary team.

XVIII.

Th' exploit of strength, dexterity, or speed,
To him nor vanity nor joy could bring.
His heart, from cruel sport estranged, would bleed
To work the wo of any living thing,
By trap, or net; by arrow, or by sling;
These he detested, those he scorn'd to wield:
He wish'd to be the guardian, not the king,
Tyrant far less, or traitor of the field.
And sure the sylvan reign unbloody joy might yield.

XIX.

Lo! where the stripling, wrapt in wonder, roves
Beneath the precipice o'erhung with pine;
And sees, on high, amidst th' encircling groves,
From cliff to cliff the foaming torrents shine:
While waters, woods, and winds, in concert join,
And Echo swells the chorus to the skies.
Would Edwin this majestic scene resign
For aught the huntsman's puny craft supplies?
Ah! no: he better knows great Nature's charms to prize.

XX.

And oft he traced the uplands, to survey,
When o'er the sky advaned th e kindling dawn,
The crimson cloud, blue main, and mountain grey,
And lake, dim-gleaming on the smoky lawn;
Far to the west the long long vale withdrawn,
Where twilight loves to linger for a while;
And now he faintly kens the bounding fawn,
And villager abroad at early toil.
But, lo! the sun appears! and heaven, earth, ocean, smile.

XXI.

And oft the craggy cliff he loved to climb,
When all in mist the world below was lost.
What dreadful pleasure! there to stand sublime,
Like shipwreck'd mariner on desert coast,
And view th' enormous waste of vapour, tost
In billows, lengthening to th' horizon round,
Now scoop'd in gulfs, with mountains now embofs'd!
And hear the voice of mirth and song rebound,
Flocks, herds, and waterfalls, along the hoar profound!

XXII.

In truth he was a strange and wayward wight,
Fond of each gentle, and each dreadful scene.
In darkness, and in storm, he found delight:
Nor less, than when on ocean-wave serene
The southern sun diffused his dazzling shene *
Even sad vicissitude amused his soul:
And if a sigh would sometimes intervene,
And down his cheek a tear of pity roll,
A sigh, a tear, so sweet, he wish'd not to control.

XXIII.

' O ye wild groves, O where is now your bloom!'
(The Muse interprets thus his tender thought.)
' Your flowers, your verdure, and your balmy
    gloom,
' Of late so grateful in the hour of drought!
' Why do the birds, that song and rapture brought
' To all your bowers, their mansions now forsake?
' Ah! why has fickle chance this ruin wrought?
' For now the storm howls mournful through the
    ' brake,
' And the dead foliage flies in many a shapeless flake.

---

* Brightness, splendour. The word is used by some late writers, as well as by Milton.

XXIV.

' Where now the rill, melodious, pure, and cool,
' And meads, with life, and mirth, and beauty
   ' crown'd!
' Ah! see, th' unsightly slime, and sluggish pool,
' Have all the solitary vale imbrown'd;
' Fled each fair form, and mute each melting
   ' sound.
' The raven croaks forlorn on naked spray.
' And, hark! the river, bursting every mound,
' Down the vale thunders; and with wasteful sway
' Uproots the grove, and rolls the shatter'd rocks
   ' away.

XXV.

' Yet such the destiny of all on earth:
' So flourishes and fades majestic man.
' Fair is the bud his vernal morn brings forth,
' And fostering gales a while the nursling fan.
' O smile, ye heavens, serene; ye mildews wan,
' Ye blighting whirlwinds, spare his balmy prime,
' Nor lessen of his life the little span.
' Born on the swift, though silent, wings of Time,
' Old age comes on apace to ravage all the clime.

XXVI.

'And be it so. Let those deplore their doom,
'Whose hope still grovels in this dark sojourn.
'But lofty souls, who look beyond the tomb,
'Can smile at Fate, and wonder how they mourn.
'Shall spring to these sad scenes no more return?
'Is yonder wave the sun's eternal bed?
'Soon shall the orient with new lustre burn,
'And spring shall soon her vital influence shed,
'Again attune the grove, again adorn the mead.

XXVII.

'Shall I be left forgotten in the dust,
'When Fate, relenting, lets the flower revive?
'Shall nature's voice, to man alone unjust,
'Bid him, though doom'd to perish, hope to live?
'Is it for this fair Virtue oft must strive
'With disappointment, penury, and pain?
'No: Heaven's immortal spring shall yet arrive;
'And man's majestic beauty bloom again,
Bright through th' eternal year of Love's trium-
'phant reign,

XXVIII.

This truth sublime his simple fire had taught.
In sooth, 'twas almost all the shepherd knew.
No subtle nor superfluous lore he sought,
Nor ever wish'd his Edwin to pursue.
' Let man's own sphere (said he) confine his view,
' Be man's peculiar work his sole delight.'
And much, and oft, he warn'd him, to eschew
Falsehood and guile, and aye maintain the right,
By pleasure unseduced, unawed by lawless might.

XXIX.

' And, from the prayer of Want, and plaint of Wo,
' O never, never turn away thine ear!
' Forlorn, in this bleak wilderness below,
' Ah! what were man, should Heaven refuse to
    ' hear!
' To others do (the law is not severe)
' What to thyself thou wishest to be done.
' Forgive thy foes; and love thy parents dear,
' And friends, and native land; nor those alone;
' All human weal and wo learn thou to make thine
    ' own.'

XXX.

See, in the rear of the warm funny fhower,
The vifionary boy from fhelter fly!
For now the ftorm of fummer-rain is o'er,
And cool, and frefh, and fragrant is the fky.
And, lo! in the dark eaft, expanded high,
The rainbow brightens to the fetting fun!
Fond fool, that deem'ft the ftreaming glory nigh,
How vain the chace thine ardor has begun!
'Tis fled afar, ere half thy purpofed race be run.

XXXI.

Yet couldft thou learn, that thus it fares with age,
When pleafure, wealth, or power the bofom warm,
This baffled hope might tame thy manhood's rage,
And Difappointment of her fting difarm.
But why fhould forefight thy fond heart alarm?
Perifh the lore that deadens young defire!
Purfue, poor imp, th' imaginary charm,
Indulge gay Hope, and Fancy's pleafing fire:
Fancy and Hope too foon fhall of themfelves expire.

XXXII.

When the long-founding curfew from afar
Loaded with loud lament the lonely gale,
Young Edwin, lighted by the evening ſtar,
Lingering and liſtening wander'd down the vale.
There would he dream of graves, and corſes pale;
And ghoſts that to the charnel-dungeon throng,
And drag a length of clanking chain, and wail,
Till ſilenced by the owl's terrific ſong,
Or blaſt that ſhrieks by fits the ſhuddering iſles along.

XXXIII.

Or, when the ſetting moon, in crimſon dyed,
Hung o'er the dark and melancholy deep,
To haunted ſtream, remote from man, he hied,
Where Fays of yore their revels wont to keep;
And there let Fancy rove at large, till ſleep
A viſion brought to his intranced ſight.
And firſt, a wildly murmuring wind 'gan creep
Shrill to his ringing ear; then tapers bright,
With inſtantaneous gleam, illumed the vault of
night.

XXXIV.

Anon in view a portal's blazon'd arch
Arose; the trumpet bids the valves unfold;
And forth an hoft of little warriors march,
Grafping the diamond lance, and targe of gold.
Their look was gentle, their demeanour bold,
And green their helms, and green their filk attire;
And here and there, right venerably old,
The long-robed minftrels wake the warbling wire,
And fome with mellow breath the martial pipe
    infpire.

XXXV.

With merriment, and fong, and timbrels clear,
A troop of dames from myrtle bowers advance;
The little warriors doff the targe and fpear,
And loud enlivening ftrains provoke the dance.
They meet, they dart away, they wheel afkance;
To right, to left, they thrid the flying maze;
Now bound aloft with vigorous fpring, then glance
Rapid along: with many-colour'd rays
Of tapers, gems, and gold, the echoing forefts blaze.

XXXVI.

The dream is fled. Proud harbinger of day,
Who scar'dst the vision with thy clarion shrill,
Fell chanticleer! who oft hast reft away
My fancied good, and brought substantial ill!
O to thy cursed scream, discordant still,
Let harmony aye shut her gentle ear:
Thy boastful mirth let jealous rivals spill,
Insult thy crest, and glossy pinions tear,
And ever in thy dreams the ruthless fox appear.

XXXVII.

Forbear, my Muse. Let Love attune thy line.
Revoke the spell. Thine Edwin frets not so.
For how should he at wicked chance repine,
Who feels from every change amusement flow?
Even now his eyes with smiles of rapture glow,
As on he wanders through the scenes of morn,
Where the fresh flowers in living lustre blow,
Where thousand pearls the dewy lawns adorn,
A thousand notes of joy in every breeze are born.

XXXVIII.

But who the melodies of morn can tell?
The wild brook babbling down the mountain side;
The lowing herd; the sheepfold's simple bell;
The pipe of early shepherd dim descried
In the lone valley; echoing far and wide
The clamorous horn along the cliffs above;
The hollow murmur of the ocean-tide;
The hum of bees, and linnet's lay of love,
And the full choir that wakes the universal grove.

XXXIX.

The cottage-curs at early pilgrim bark;
Crown'd with her pail the tripping milkmaid sings;
The whistling plowman stalks afield; and, hark!
Down the rough slope the ponderous waggon rings;
Through rustling corn the hare astonish'd springs;
Slow tolls the village-clock the drowsy hour;
The partridge bursts away on whirring wings;
Deep mourns the turtle in sequester'd bower,
And shrill lark carols clear from her aërial tour.

XL.

O Nature, how in every charm supreme!
Whose votaries feast on raptures ever new!
O for the voice and fire of seraphim,
To sing thy glories with devotion due!
Blest be the day I 'scaped the wrangling crew,
From Pyrrho's maze, and Epicurus' sty;
And held high converse with the godlike few,
Who to th' enraptur'd heart, and ear, and eye,
Teach beauty, virtue, truth, and love, and melody.

XLI.

Hence! ye, who snare and stupefy the mind,
Sophists, of beauty, virtue, joy, the bane!
Greedy and fell, though impotent and blind,
Who spread your filthy nets in Truth's fair fane,
And ever ply your venom'd fangs amain!
Hence to dark Error's den, whose rankling slime
First gave you form! hence! lest the Muse should deign,
(Though loath on theme so mean to waste a rhyme),
With vengeance to pursue your sacrilegious crime.

XLII.

But hail, ye mighty masters of the lay,
Nature's true sons, the friends of man and truth!
Whose song, sublimely sweet, serenely gay,
Amused my childhood, and inform'd my youth.
O let your spirit still my bosom sooth,
Inspire my dreams, and my wild wanderings guide:
Your voice each rugged path of life can smooth;
For well I know, where-ever ye reside,
There harmony, and peace, and innocence abide.

XLIII.

Ah me! neglected on the lonesome plain,
As yet poor Edwin never knew your lore,
Save when against the winter's drenching rain,
And driving snow, the cottage shut the door.
Then, as instructed by tradition hoar,
Her legend when the Beldame 'gan impart,
Or chant the old heroic ditty o'er,
Wonder and joy ran thrilling to his heart;
Much he the tale admired, but more the tuneful art.

XLIV.

Various and strange was the long-winded tale;
And halls, and knights, and feats of arms, dis-
 play'd;
Or merry swains, who quaff the nut-brown ale,
And sing, enamour'd of the nut-brown maid;
The moon-light revel of the fairy glade;
Or hags, that suckle an infernal brood,
And ply in caves th' unutterable trade*,
'Midst fiends and spectres, quench the moon in
 blood,
Yell in the midnight storm, or ride th' infuriate flood.

XLV.

But when to horror his amazement rose,
A gentler strain the Beldame would rehearse,
A tale of rural life, a tale of woes,
 The orphan-babes, and guardian uncle fierce.

---

* Allusion to SHAKESPEARE.
Macbeth. How now, ye secret, black, and midnight hags,
 What is't you do?
Witches. A deed WITHOUT A NAME.
               MACBETH, Act 4. Scene 1.

O cruel! will no pang of pity pierce
That heart by luſt of lucre fear'd to ſtone?
For ſure, if aught of virtue laſt, or verſe,
To lateſt times ſhall tender ſouls bemoan
Thoſe helpleſs orphan-babes by thy fell arts undone.

XLVI.

Behold, with berries ſmear'd, with brambles
   torn *,
The babes now famiſh'd lay them down to die.
Amidſt the howl of darkſome woods forlorn,
Folded in one another's arms they lie;
Nor friend, nor ſtranger, hears their dying cry:
'For from the town the man returns no more.'
But thou, who Heaven's juſt vengeance dareſt
   defy,
This deed with fruitleſs tears ſhalt ſoon deplore,
When Death lays waſte thy houſe, and flames con-
   ſume thy ſtore.

---

* See the fine old ballad, called, THE CHILDREN IN THE WOOD.

XLVII.

A stifled smile of stern vindictive joy
Brighten'd one moment Edwin's starting tear.
' But why should gold man's feeble mind decoy,
' And Innocence thus die by doom severe?'
O Edwin! while thy heart is yet sincere,
Th' assaults of discontent and doubt repel:
Dark even at noontide is our mortal sphere;
But let us hope; to doubt is to rebel;
Let us exult in hope, that all shall yet be well.

XLVIII.

Nor be thy generous indignation check'd,
Nor check'd the tender tear to Misery given;
From Guilt's contagious power shall that protect,
This soften and refine the soul for Heaven.
But dreadful is their doom, whom doubt has driven
To censure Fate, and pious hope forego:
Like yonder blasted boughs by lightning riven,
Perfection, beauty, life, they never know,
But frown on all that pass, a monument of wo.

XLIX.

Shall he, whose birth, maturity, and age,
Scarce fill the circle of one summer day,
Shall the poor gnat with discontent and rage
Exclaim, that Nature hastens to decay,
If but a cloud obstruct the solar ray,
If but a momentary shower descend!
Or shall frail man Heaven's dread decree gainsay,
Which bade the series of events extend
Wide through unnumber'd worlds, and ages without end!

L.

One part, one little part, we dimly scan
Through the dark medium of life's feverish dream;
Yet dare arraign the whole stupendous plan,
If but that little part incongruous seem,
Nor is that part perhaps what mortals deem;
Oft from apparent ill our blessings rise.
O then renounce that impious self-esteem,
That aims to trace the secrets of the skies:
For thou art but of dust; be humble, and be wise.

LI.

Thus Heaven enlarged his foul in riper years.
For Nature gave him strength and fire, to soar
On Fancy's wing above this vale of tears;
Where dark cold-hearted sceptics, creeping, pore
Through microscope of metaphysic lore:
And much they grope for truth, but never hit.
For why? their powers, inadequate before,
This idle art makes more and more unfit;
Yet deem they darkness light, and their vain blunders wit.

LII.

Nor was this ancient dame a foe to mirth.
Her ballad, jest, and riddle's quaint device
Oft cheer'd the shepherds round their social hearth;
Whom levity or spleen could ne'er entice
To purchase chat or laughter, at the price
Of decency. Nor let it faith exceed,
That Nature forms a rustic taste so nice.
Ah! had they been of court or city breed,
Such delicacy were right marvellous indeed.

LIII.

Oft, when the winter-storm had ceased to rave,
He roam'd the snowy waste at even, to view
The cloud stupendous, from th' Atlantic wave
High-towering, sail along th' horizon blue:
Where 'midst the changeful scenery ever new
Fancy a thousand wondrous forms descries
More wildly great than ever pencil drew,
  Rocks, torrents, gulfs, and shapes of giant size,
And glittering cliffs on cliffs, and fiery ramparts rise.

LIV.

Thence musing onward to the sounding shore
The lone enthusiast oft would take his way,
Listening with pleasing dread to the deep roar
Of the wide-weltering waves. In black array
When sulphurous clouds roll'd on th' autumnal day,
Even then he hasten'd from the haunt of man,
Along the trembling wilderness to stray,
  What time the lightning's fierce career began,
And o'er Heaven's rending arch the rattling thunder ran.

LV.

Refponfive to the fprightly pipe when all
In fprightly dance the village-youth were join'd,
Edwin, of melody aye held in thrall,
From the rude gambol far remote reclined,
Sooth'd with the foft notes warbling in the wind.
Ah then, all jollity feem'd noife and folly.
To the pure foul by Fancy's fire refined,
Ah what is mirth but turbulence unholy,
When with the charm compared of heavenly melancholy!

LVI.

Is there a heart that mufic cannot melt?
Alas! how is that rugged heart forlorn!
Is there, who ne'er thofe myftic tranfports felt
Of folitude and melancholy born?
He needs not woo the Mufe; he is her fcorn.
The fophift's rope of cobweb he fhall twine;
Mope o'er the fchoolman's peevifh page; or mourn,
And delve for life, in Mammon's dirty mine;
Sneak with the fcoundrel fox, or grunt with glutton fwine.

LVII.

For Edwin Fate a nobler doom had plann'd;
Song was his favourite and firſt purſuit.
The wild harp rang to his adventurous hand,
And languiſh'd to his breath the plaintive flute.
His infant muſe, though artleſs, was not mute:
Of elegance as yet he took no care;
For this of time and culture is the fruit;
And Edwin gain'd at laſt this fruit ſo rare:
As in ſome future verſe I purpoſe to declare.

LVIII.

Meanwhile, whate'er of beautiful, or new,
Sublime, or dreadful, in earth, ſea, or ſky,
By chance, or ſearch, was offer'd to his view,
He ſcan'd with curious and romantic eye.
Whate'er of lore tradition could ſupply
From Gothic tale, or ſong, or fable old,
Rouſed him, ſtill keen to liſten and to pry.
At laſt, though long by penury control'd,
And ſolitude, his ſoul her graces 'gan unfold.

LIX.

Thus on the chill Lapponian's dreary land,
For many a long month loft in fnow profound,
When Sol from Cancer fends the feafon bland,
And in their northern cave the ftorms are bound;
From filent mountains, ftraight, with ftartling found,
Torrents are hurl'd; green hills emerge; and lo,
The trees with foliage, cliffs with flowers are crown'd;
Pure rills through vales of verdure warbling go;
And wonder, love, and joy, the peafant's heart o'erflow *.

LX.

Here paufe, my Gothic lyre, a little while.
The leifure hour is all that thou canft claim.
But on this verfe if MONTAGU fhould fmile,
New ftrains erelong fhall animate thy frame.

---

* Spring and Autumn are hardly known to the Laplanders. About the time the Sun enters Cancer, their fields, which a week before were covered with fnow, appear on a fudden full of grafs and flowers.
SCHEFFER's Hiftory of Lapland, p. 16.

And her applaufe to me is more than fame;
For ftill with truth accords her tafte refined.
At lucre or renown let others aim,
I only wifh to pleafe the gentle mind,
Whom nature's charms infpire, and love of human-
kind.

THE MINSTREL;

OR, THE

PROGRESS OF GENIUS.

THE SECOND BOOK.

I.

OF chance or change O let not man complain,
  Elſe ſhall he never never ceaſe to wail;
For, from the imperial dome, to where the ſwain
Rears the lone cottage in the ſilent dale,
All feel th' aſſault of fortune's fickle gale;
Art, empire, earth itſelf, to change are doom'd;
Earthquakes have raiſed to heaven the humble vale,
And gulphs the mountain's mighty maſs entomb'd,
And where th' Atlantick rolls wide continents have bloom'd *.

* See PLATO's Timeus.

II.

But sure to foreign climes we need not range,
Nor search the ancient records of our race,
To learn the dire effects of time and change,
Which in ourselves, alas, we daily trace.
Yet at the darken'd eye, the wither'd face,
Or hoary hair, I never will repine:
But spare, O Time, whate'er of mental grace,
Of candour, love, or sympathy divine,
Whate'er of fancy's ray, or friendship's flame is mine.

III.

So I, obsequious to Truth's dread command,
Shall here without reluctance change my lay,
And smite the Gothic lyre with harsher hand;
Now when I leave that flowery path for aye
Of childhood, where I sported many a day,
Warbling and sauntering carelesly along;
Where every face was innocent and gay,
Each vale romantic, tuneful every tongue,
Sweet, wild, and artless all, as Edwin's infant song.

IV.

" Perish the lore that deadens young desire"
Is the soft tenor of my song no more.
Edwin, though loved of heaven, must not aspire
To bliss, which mortals never knew before.
On trembling wings let youthful fancy soar,
Nor always haunt the sunny realms of joy:
But now and then the shades of life explore;
Though many a sound and sight of woe annoy,
And many a qualm of care his rising hopes destroy.

V.

Vigour from toil, from trouble patience grows.
The weakly blossom, warm in summer bower,
Some tints of transient beauty may disclose;
But soon it withers in the chilling hour.
Mark yonder oaks! Superiour to the power
Of all the warring winds of heaven they rise,
And from the stormy promontory tower,
And toss their giant arms amid the skies,
While each assailing blast increase of strength sup-
    plies.

VI.

And now the downy cheek and deepen'd voice
Gave dignity to Edwin's blooming prime;
And walks of wider circuit were his choice,
And vales more wild, and mountains more sublime.
One evening, as he framed the careless rhyme,
It was his chance to wander far abroad,
And o'er a lonely eminence to climb,
Which heretofore his foot had never trode;
A vale appear'd below, a deep retired abode.

VII.

Thither he hied, enamour'd of the scene.
For rocks on rocks piled, as by magic spell,
Here scorch'd with lightning, there with ivy green,
Fenced from the north and east this savage dell.
Southward a mountain rose with easy swell,
Whose long long groves eternal murmur made:
And toward the western sun a streamlet fell,
Where, through the cliffs, the eye, remote, survey'd
Blue hills, and glittering waves, and skies in gold array'd.

VIII.

Along this narrow valley you might fee
The wild deer fporting on the meadow ground,
And, here and there, a folitary tree,
Or mossy ftone, or rock with woodbine crown'd.
Oft did the cliffs reverberate the found
Of parted fragments tumbling from on high;
And from the fummit of that craggy mound
The perching eagle oft was heard to cry,
Or on refounding wings to fhoot athwart the fky.

IX.

One cultivated fpot there was, that fpread
Its flowery bofom to the noonday beam,
Where many a rofe-bud rears its blufhing head,
And herbs for food with future plenty teem.
Sooth'd by the lulling found of grove and ftream,
Romantick vifions fwarm on Edwin's foul:
He minded not the fun's laft trembling gleam,
Nor heard from far the twilight curfew toll;
When flowly on his ear thefe moving accents ftole.

X.

‘ Hail, awful scenes, that calm the troubled breast,
‘ And woo the weary to profound repose;
‘ Can passion's wildest uproar lay to rest,
‘ And whisper comfort to the man of woes!
‘ Here Innocence may wander, safe from foes,
‘ And Contemplation soar on seraph wings.
‘ O Solitude, the man who thee foregoes,
‘ When lucre lures him, or ambition stings,
‘ Shall never know the source whence real grandeur
    ‘ springs.

XI.

‘ Vain man, is grandeur given to gay attire?
‘ Then let the butterfly thy pride upbraid:
‘ To friends, attendants, armies, bought with hire?
‘ It is thy weakness that requires their aid:
‘ To palaces, with gold and gems inlay'd?
‘ They fear the thief, and tremble in the storm:
‘ To hosts, through carnage who to conquest wade?
‘ Behold the victor vanquish'd by the worm!
‘ Behold, what deeds of woe the locust can perform!

XII.

'True dignity is his, whose tranquil mind
'Virtue has raised above the things below;
'Who, every hope and fear to heaven resign'd,
'Shrinks not, though Fortune aim her deadliest
  'blow.'
This strain from 'midst the rocks was heard to flow,
In solemn sounds. Now beam'd the evening star;
And from embattled clouds emerging slow
Cynthia came riding on her silver car;
And hoary mountain-cliffs shone faintly from afar.

XIII.

Soon did the solemn voice its theme renew;
(While Edwin wrapt in wonder listening stood)
'Ye tools and toys of tyranny, adieu,
'Scorn'd by the wise, and hated by the good!
'Ye only can engage the servile brood
'Of Levity and Lust, who all their days,
'Asham'd of truth and liberty, have woo'd,
'And hug'd the chain, that glittering on their gaze
'Seems to outshine the pomp of heaven's empyreal
  'blaze.

XIV.

' Like them, abandon'd to Ambition's sway,
' I fought for glory in the paths of guile;
' And fawn'd and smiled, to plunder and betray,
' Myself betray'd and plunder'd all the while;
' So gnaw'd the viper the corroding file.
' But now with pangs of keen remorse I rue
' Those years of trouble and debasement vile.
' Yet why should I this cruel theme pursue!
' Fly, fly, detested thoughts, for ever, from my
  ' view.

XV.

' The gusts of appetite, the clouds of care,
' And storms of disappointment, all o'erpast,
' Henceforth no earthly hope with heaven shall
  ' share
' This heart, where peace serenely shines at last.
' And if for me no treasure be amass'd,
' And if no future age shall hear my name,
' I lurk the more secure from fortune's blast,
' And with more leisure feed this pious flame,
' Whose rapture far transcends the fairest hopes of
  ' fame.

XVI.

'The end and the reward of toil is reft.
'Be all my prayer for virtue and for peace.
'Of wealth and fame, of pomp and power poffefs'd,
'Who ever felt his weight of woe decreafe!
'Ah! what avails the lore of Rome and Greece,
'The lay heaven-prompted, and harmonious
    'ftring,
'The duft of Ophir, or the Tyrian fleece,
'All that art, fortune, enterprife, can bring,
'If envy, fcorn, remorfe, or pride the bofom wring!

XVII.

'Let Vanity adorn the marble tomb
'With trophies, rhymes, and fcutcheons of
    'renown,
'In the deep dungeon of fome Gothic dome,
'Where night and defolation ever frown.
'Mine be the breezy hill that fkirts the down;
'Where a green graffy turf is all I crave,
'With here and there a violet beftrown,
'Faft by a brook, or fountain's murmuring wave;
'And many an evening fun fhine fweetly on my
    'grave.

XVIII.

' And thither let the village swain repair;
' And, light of heart, the village maiden gay,
' To deck with flowers her half-dishevel'd hair,
' And celebrate the merry morn of May.
' There let the shepherd's pipe the live-long day
' Fill all the grove with love's bewitching wo;
' And when mild Evening comes in mantle grey,
' Let not the blooming band make haste to go;
' No ghost nor spell my long and last abode shall
  ' know.

XIX.

' For though I fly to scape from Fortune's rage,
' And bear the scars of envy, spite, and scorn,
' Yet with mankind no horrid war I wage,
' Yet with no impious spleen my breast is torn:
' For virtue lost, and ruin'd man, I mourn.
' O Man, creation's pride, heaven's darling child,
' Whom nature's best divinest gifts adorn,
' Why from thy home are truth and joy exiled,
' And all thy favourite haunts with blood and tears
  ' defiled!

XX.

'Along yon glittering sky what glory streams!
'What majesty attends Night's lovely queen!
'Fair laugh our vallies in the vernal beams;
'And mountains rise, and oceans roll between,
'And all conspire to beautify the scene.
'But, in the mental world, what chaos drear!
'What forms of mournful, loathsome, furious
  'mien!
'O when shall that Eternal Morn appear,
'These dreadful forms to chase, this chaos dark to
  'clear!

XXI.

'O Thou, at whose creative smile, yon heaven,
'In all the pomp of beauty, life, and light,
'Rose from th' abyss; when dark Confusion, driven
'Down down the bottomless profound of night,
'Fled, where he ever flies thy piercing sight!
'O glance on these sad shades one pitying ray,
'To blast the fury of oppressive might,
'Melt the hard heart to love and mercy's sway,
'And cheer the wandering soul, and light him on
  the way.'

XXII.

Silence enfued: and Edwin raifed his eyes
In tears, for grief lay heavy at his heart.
‘ And is it thus in courtly life (he cries)
‘ That man to man acts a betrayer's part?
‘ And dares he thus the gifts of heaven pervert,
‘ Each focial inftinct, and fublime defire?
‘ Hail poverty! if honour, wealth, and art,
‘ If what the great purfue, and learn'd admire,
‘ Thus diffipate and quench the foul's ethereal fire!'

XXIII.

He faid, and turn'd away; nor did the Sage
O'erhear, in filent orifons employ'd.
The Youth, his rifing forrow to affuage,
Home as he hied, the evening fcene enjoy'd:
For now no cloud obfcures the ftarry void;
The yellow moonlight fleeps on all the hills * ;
Nor is the mind with ftartling founds annoy'd;
A foothing murmur the lone region fills,
Of groves, and dying gales, and melancholy rills.

---

* How fweet the moonlight fleeps upon this bank.
SHAKESPEARE.

XXIV.

But he from day to day more anxious grew.
The voice still seem'd to vibrate on his ear.
Nor durst he hope the Hermit's tale untrue;
For man he seem'd to love, and heaven to fear;
And none speaks false, where there is none to hear.
' Yet can man's gentle heart become so fell!
' No more in vain conjecture let me wear
' My hours away, but seek the Hermit's cell;
' 'Tis he my doubt can clear, perhaps my care
 ' dispel.'

XXV.

At early dawn the Youth his journey took,
And many a mountain pass'd, and valley wide,
Then reach'd the wild; where, in a flowery nook,
And seated on a mossy stone, he spied
An antient man: his harp lay him beside.
A stag sprang from the pasture at his call,
And, kneeling, lick'd the wither'd hand that tied
A wreathe of woodbine round his antlers tall,
And hung his lofty neck with many a flowret small.

XXVI.

And now the hoary Sage arose, and saw
The wanderer approaching: innocence
Smiled on his glowing cheek, but modest awe
Deprefs'd his eye, that fear'd to give offence.
' Who art thou, courteous stranger ? and from
    ' whence ?
' Why roam thy steps to this sequester'd dale ?'
' A shepherd-boy (the Youth replied), far hence
' My habitation; hear my artless tale;
' Nor levity nor falsehood shall thine ear assail.

XXVII.

' Late as I roam'd, intent on Nature's charms,
' I reach'd at eve this wilderness profound;
' And, leaning where yon oak expands her arms,
' Heard these rude cliffs thine awful voice re-
    ' bound ;
' (For in thy speech I recognise the sound).
' You mourn'd for ruin'd man, and virtue lost,
' And seem'd to feel of keen remorse the wound,
' Pondering on former days by guilt engross'd,
' Or in the giddy storm of dissipation toss'd.

XXVIII.

' But say, in courtly life can craft be learn'd,
' Where knowledge opens, and exalts the soul?
' Where Fortune lavishes her gifts unearn'd,
' Can selfishness the liberal heart control?
' Is glory there achiev'd by arts, as foul
' As those that felons, fiends, and furies plan?
' Spiders ensnare, snakes poison, tygers prowl;
' Love is the godlike attribute of man.
' O teach a simple youth this mystery to scan.

XXIX.

' Or else the lamentable strain disclaim,
' And give me back the calm, contented mind;
' Which, late, exulting, view'd in Nature's frame,
' Goodness untainted, wisdom unconfined,
' Grace, grandeur, and utility combined.
' Restore those tranquil days, that saw me still
' Well pleased with all, but most with humankind;
' When fancy roved through Nature's works at
  ' will,
' Uncheck'd by cold distrust, and uninform'd of ill.'

XXX.

‘ Wouldſt thou (the Sage replied) in peace return
‘ To the gay dreams of fond romantick youth,
‘ Leave me to hide, in this remote ſojourn,
‘ From every gentle ear the dreadful truth:
‘ For, if my deſultory ſtrain with ruth
‘ And indignation make thine eyes o'erflow,
‘ Alas! what comfort could thy anguiſh ſooth,
‘ Shouldſt thou th' extent of human folly know.
‘ Be ignorance thy choice, where knowledge leads
  ‘ to wo.

XXXI.

‘ But let untender thoughts afar be driven;
‘ Nor venture to arraign the dread decree.
‘ For know, to man, as candidate for heaven,
‘ The voice of The Eternal ſaid, Be free:
‘ And this divine prerogative to thee
‘ Does virtue, happineſs, and heaven convey;
‘ For virtue is the child of liberty,
‘ And happineſs of virtue; nor can they
‘ Be free to keep the path, who are not free to ſtray.

XXXII.

'Yet leave me not. I would allay that grief,
'Which else might thy young virtue overpower;
'And in thy converse I shall find relief,
'When the dark shades of melancholy lower;
'For solitude has many a dreary hour,
'Even when exempt from grief, remorse, and pain:
'Come often then; for, haply, in my bower,
'Amusement, knowledge, wisdom thou may'st
   'gain:
'If I one soul improve, I have not lived in vain.'

XXXIII.

And now, at length, to Edwin's ardent gaze
The Muse of history unrolls her page.
But few, alas! the scenes her art displays,
To charm his fancy, or his heart engage.
Here Chiefs their thirst of power in blood assuage,
And straight their flames with tenfold fierceness
   burn:
Here smiling Virtue prompts the patriot's rage,
But lo, erelong, is left alone to mourn,
And languish in the dust, and clasp th' abandon'd urn.

XXXIV.

' Ambition's flippery verge fhall mortals tread,
' Where ruin's gulph unfathom'd yawns beneath!
' Shall life, fhall liberty be loft, (he faid)
' For the vain toys that Pomp and Power bequeath!
' The car of victory, the plume, the wreathe,
' Defend not from the bolt of fate the brave;
' No note the clarion of Renown can breathe,
' T' alarm the long night of the lonely grave,
' Or check the headlong hafte of Time's o'er-
 ' whelming wave.

XXXV.

' Ah, what avails it to have traced the fprings
' That whirl of empire the ftupendous wheel!
' Ah, what have I to do with conquering kings,
' Hands drench'd in blood, and breafts begirt
 ' with fteel!
' To thofe, whom Nature taught to think and feel,
' Heroes, alas! are things of fmall concern;
' Could Hiftory man's fecret heart reveal,
' And what imports a heaven-born mind to learn,
' Her tranfcripts to explore what bofom would not
 ' yearn!

XXXVI.

' This praise, O Cheronean Sage *, is thine.
' (Why should this praise to thee alone belong!)
' All else from Nature's moral path decline,
' Lured by the toys that captivate the throng;
' To herd in cabinets and camps, among
' Spoil, carnage, and the cruel pomp of pride;
' Or chaunt of heraldry the drowsy song,
' How tyrant blood, o'er many a region wide,
' Rolls to a thousand thrones its execrable tide.

XXXVII.

' O who of man the story will unfold,
' Ere victory and empire wrought annoy,
' In that elysian age (misnamed of gold)
' The age of love, and innocence, and joy,
' When all were great and free! man's sole employ
' To deck the bosom of his parent earth;
' Or toward his bower the murmuring stream decoy,
' To aid the floweret's long-expected birth,
' And lull the bed of peace, and crown the board
  ' of mirth.

* PLUTARCH.

XXXVIII.

' Sweet were your shades, O ye primeval groves,
' Whose boughs to man his food and shelter lent,
' Pure in his pleasures, happy in his loves,
' His eye still smiling, and his heart content.
' Then, hand in hand, Health, Sport, and Labour went.
' Nature supply'd the wish she taught to crave.
' None prowl'd for prey, none watch'd to circumvent.
' To all an equal lot Heaven's bounty gave:
' No vassal fear'd his lord, no tyrant fear'd his slave.

XXXIX.

' But ah! th' Historick Muse has never dared
' To pierce those hallow'd bowers; 'tis Fancy's beam
' Pour'd on the vision of th' enraptured Bard,
' That paints the charms of that delicious theme.
' Then hail sweet Fancy's ray! and hail the dream
' That weans the weary soul from guilt and woe!
' Careless what others of my choice may deem,
' I long where Love and Fancy lead to go,
' And meditate on heaven; enough of earth I know.

XL.

' I cannot blame thy choice (the Sage replied)
' For soft and smooth are Fancy's flowery ways.
' And yet, even there, if left without a guide,
' The young adventurer unsafely plays.
' Eyes dazzled long by Fiction's gaudy rays
' In modest Truth no light nor beauty find.
' And who, my child, would trust the meteor-blaze,
' That soon must fail, and leave the wanderer
 ' blind,
' More dark and helpless far, than if it ne'er had
 ' shined?

XLI.

' Fancy enervates, while it sooths, the heart,
' And, while it dazzles, wounds the mental sight:
' To joy each heightening charm it can impart,
' But wraps the hour of wo in tenfold night.
' And often, where no real ills affright,
' Its visionary fiends, an endless train,
' Assail with equal or superior might,
' And through the throbbing heart, and dizzy
 ' brain,
' And shivering nerves, shoot stings of more than
 ' mortal pain.

XLII.

' And yet, alas, the real ills of life
' Claim the full vigour of a mind prepared,
' Prepared for patient, long, laborious strife,
' Its guide Experience, and Truth its guard.
' We fare on earth as other men have fared.
' Were they succefsful? Let not us defpair.
' Was difappointment oft their sole reward?
' Yet shall their tale instruct, if it declare,
' How they have borne the load ourselves are doom'd
    ' to bear.

XLIII.

' What charms th' Historick Muse adorn, from
    ' spoils,
' And blood, and tyrants, when she wings her flight,
' To hail the patriot Prince, whose pious toils
' Sacred to science, liberty, and right,
' And peace, through every age divinely bright
' Shall shine the boast and wonder of mankind!
' Sees yonder sun, from his meridian height,
' A lovelier scene, than Virtue thus inshrined
' In power, and man with man for mutual aid
    ' combined?

XLIV.

' Hail sacred Polity, by Freedom rear'd!
' Hail sacred Freedom, when by Law restrain'd!
' Without you what were man? A groveling herd
' In darkness, wretchedness, and want enchain'd.
' Sublimed by you, the Greek and Roman reign'd
' In arts unrival'd: O, to latest days,
' In Albion may your influence unprofaned
' To godlike worth the generous bosom raise,
' And prompt the Sage's lore, and fire the poet's
   ' lays!

XLV.

' But now let other themes our care engage.
' For lo, with modest yet majestick grace,
' To curb Imagination's lawless rage,
' And from within the cherish'd heart to brace,
' Philosophy appears. The gloomy race
' By Indolence and moping Fancy bred,
' Fear, Discontent, Solicitude give place,
' And Hope and Courage brighten in their stead,
' While on the kindling soul her vital beams are
   ' shed.

XLVI.

' Then waken from long lethargy to life *
' The seeds of happiness, and powers of thought;
' Then jarring appetites forego their strife,
' A strife by ignorance to madness wrought.
' Pleasure by savage man is dearly bought
' With fell revenge, lust that defies controul,
' With gluttony and death. The mind untaught
' Is a dark waste, where fiends and tempests howl;
' As Phebus to the world, is Science to the soul.

XLVII.

' And Reason now through Number, Time, and
 ' Space,
' Darts the keen lustre of her serious eye,
' And learns, from facts compared, the laws to trace,
' Whose long progression leads to Deity.
' Can mortal strength presume to soar so high!
' Can mortal sight, so oft bedim'd with tears,
' Such glory bear!—for lo, the shadows fly
' From nature's face; Confusion disappears,
' And order charms the eyes, and harmony the ears.

---

 * The influence of the Philosophick Spirit, in humanizing the mind, and preparing it for intellectual exertion and delicate pleasure;—in exploring, by the help of geometry, the system of the

XLVIII.

' In the deep windings of the grove, no more
' The hag obscene, and griesly phantom dwell;
' Nor in the fall of mountain-stream, or roar
' Of winds, is heard the angry spirit's yell;
' No wizard mutters the tremendous spell,
' Nor sinks convulsive in prophetick swoon;
' Nor bids the noise of drums and trumpets swell,
' To ease of fancied pangs the labouring moon,
' Or chace the shade that blots the blazing orb of noon.

XLIX.

' Many a long-lingering year, in lonely isle,
' Stun'd with th' eternal turbulence of waves,
' Lo, with dim eyes, that never learn'd to smile,
' And trembling hands, the famish'd native
  ' craves
' Of Heaven his wretched fare: shivering in caves,
' Or scorch'd on rocks, he pines from day to day;
' But Science gives the word; and lo, he braves
' The surge and tempest, lighted by her ray,
' And to a happier land wafts merrily away.

---

universe;—in banishing superstition;—in promoting navigation, agriculture, medicine, and moral and political science:—from Stanza XLVI. to Stanza LVI.

L.

' And even where Nature loads the teeming plain
' With the full pomp of vegetable ſtore,
' Her bounty, unimproved, is deadly bane.
' Dark woods and rankling wilds, from ſhore to
 ' ſhore,
' Stretch their enormous gloom; which to explore
' Even Fancy trembles, in her ſprightlieſt mood;
' For there, each eyeball gleams with luſt of gore,
' Neſtles each murderous and each monſtrous
 ' brood,
' Plague lurks in every ſhade, and ſteams from
 ' every flood.

LI.

' 'Twas from Philoſophy man learn'd to tame
' The ſoil by plenty to intemperance fed.
' Lo, from the echoing ax, and thundering flame,
' Poiſon and plague and yelling rage are fled.
' The waters, burſting from their ſlimy bed,
' Bring health and melody to every vale:
' And, from the breezy main, and mountain's head,
' Ceres and Flora, to the ſunny dale,
' To fan their glowing charms, invite the flutter-
 ' ing gale.

LII.

' What dire neceffities on every hand
' Our art, our ftrength, our fortitude require!
' Of foes inteftine what a numerous band
' Againft this little throb of life confpire!
' Yet Science can elude their fatal ire
' A while, and turn afide Death's level'd dart,
' Sooth the fharp pang, allay the fever's fire;
' And brace the nerves once more, and cheer the
    ' heart,
' And yet a few foft nights and balmy days impart.

LIII.

' Nor lefs to regulate man's moral frame
' Science exerts her all-compofing fway.
' Flutters thy breaft with fear, or pants for fame,
' Or pines to Indolence and Spleen a prey,
' Or Avarice, a fiend more fierce than they?
' Flee to the fhade of Academus' grove;
' Where cares moleft not, difcord melts away
' In harmony, and the pure paffions prove
' How fweet the words of truth breathed from the
    ' lips of Love.

LIV.

' What cannot Art and Induſtry perform,
' When Science plans the progreſs of their toil!
' They ſmile at penury, diſeaſe, and ſtorm;
' And oceans from their mighty mounds recoil.
' When tyrants ſcourge, or demagogues em-
 ' broil
' A land, or when the rabble's headlong rage
' Order transforms to anarchy and ſpoil,
' Deep-verſed in man the philoſophick Sage
' Prepares with lenient hand their phrenzy to
  ' aſſwage.

LV.

' 'Tis he alone, whoſe comprehenſive mind,
' From ſituation, temper, ſoil, and clime
' Explored, a nation's various powers can bind
' And various orders, in one Form ſublime
' Of policy, that, midſt the wrecks of time,
' Secure ſhall lift its head on high, nor fear
' Th' aſſault of foreign or domeſtick crime,
' While publick faith, and publick love ſincere,
' And Induſtry and Law maintain their ſway
  ' ſevere.'

LVI.

Enraptured by the Hermit's strain, the Youth
Proceeds the path of Science to explore.
And now, expanding to the beams of Truth,
New energies, and charms unknown before,
His mind disclotes: Fancy now no more
Wantons on fickle pinion through the skies;
But, fix'd in aim, and conscious of her power,
Aloft from cause to cause exults to rise,
Creation's blended stores arranging as she flies.

LVII.

Nor love of novelty alone inspires,
Their laws and nice dependencies to scan;
For, mindful of the aids that life requires,
And of the services man owes to man,
He meditates new arts on Nature's plan;
The cold desponding breast of Sloth to warm,
The flame of Industry and Genius fan,
And Emulation's noble rage alarm,
And the long hours of Toil and Solitude to charm.

LVIII.

But She, who set on fire his infant heart,
And all his dreams, and all his wanderings shared
And bless'd, the Muse, and her celestial art,
Still claim th' Enthusiast's fond and first regard.
From Nature's beauties variously compared
And variously combined, he learns to frame
Those forms of bright perfection*, which the Bard,
While boundless hopes and boundless views in-
    flame,
Enamour'd consecrates to never-dying fame.

LIX.

Of late, with cumbersome, though pompous show,
Edwin would oft his flowery rhyme deface,
Through ardour to adorn; but Nature now
To his experienced eye a modest grace
Presents, where Ornament the second place
Holds, to intrinsick worth and just design
Subservient still. Simplicity apace
Tempers his rage: he owns her charm divine,
And clears th' ambiguous phrase, and lops th' un-
    wieldy line.

---

* General ideas of excellence, the immediate archetypes of sublime imitation, both in painting and in poetry. See ARISTOTLE'S POETICKS, and THE DISCOURSES OF SIR JOSHUA REYNOLDS.

LX.

Fain would I sing (much yet unsung remains)
What sweet delirium o'er his bosom stole,
When the great Shepherd of the Mantuan plains*
His deep majestick melody 'gan roll:
Fain would I sing, what transport storm'd his soul,
How the red current throb'd his veins along,
When, like Pelides, bold beyond controul,
Without art graceful, without effort strong,
Homer raised high to heaven the loud, th' impetuous
    song.

LXI.

And how his lyre, though rude her first essays,
Now skill'd to sooth, to triumph, to complain,
Warbling at will through each harmonious maze,
Was taught to modulate the artful strain,
I fain would sing:—but ah! I strive in vain.
Sighs from a breaking heart my voice confound.
With trembling step, to join yon weeping train,
I haste, where gleams funereal glare around,
And, mix'd with shrieks of woe, the knells of death
    resound.

* VIRGIL.

LXII.

Adieu, ye lays, that Fancy's flowers adorn,
The soft amusement of the vacant mind!
He sleeps in dust, and all the Muses mourn,
He, whom each virtue fired, each grace refined,
Friend, teacher, pattern, darling of mankind!*
He sleeps in dust. Ah, how should I pursue
My theme! To heart-consuming grief resign'd
Here on his recent grave I fix my view,
And pour my bitter tears. Ye flowery lays, adieu!

LXIII.

Art thou, my GREGORY, for ever fled!
And am I left to unavailing woe!
When fortune's storms assail this weary head,
Where cares long since have shed untimely snow,
Ah, now for comfort whither shall I go!
No more thy soothing voice my anguish chears:
Thy placid eyes with smiles no longer glow,
My hopes to cherish, and allay my fears.
'Tis meet that I should mourn: flow forth afresh my
  tears.

---

* This excellent person died suddenly, on the 10th of February 1773. The conclusion of the poem was written a few days after.

RETIREMENT.

1758.

WHEN in the crimson cloud of Even
    The lingering light decays,
And Hesper on the front of heaven
    His glittering gem displays;
Deep in the silent vale, unseen,
Beside a lulling stream,
A pensive Youth, of placid mien,
Indulged this tender theme.

Ye cliffs, in hoary grandeur piled
    High o'er the glimmering dale;
Ye woods, along whose windings wild
    Murmurs the solemn gale;
Where Melancholy strays forlorn,
    And Woe retires to weep,
What time the wan moon's yellow horn,
    Gleams on the western deep:

RETIREMENT.

To you, ye waſtes, whoſe artleſs charms
Ne'er drew Ambition's eye,
Scaped a tumultuous world's alarms,
To your retreats I fly.
Deep in your moſt ſequeſter'd bower
Let me at laſt recline,
Where Solitude, mild, modeſt Power,
Leans on her ivy'd ſhrine.

How ſhall I woo thee, matchleſs Fair!
Thy heavenly ſmile how win!
Thy ſmile, that ſmooths the brow of Care,
And ſtills the ſtorm within.
O wilt thou to thy favourite grove
Thine ardent votary bring,
And bleſs his hours, and bid them move
Serene, on ſilent wing!

Oft let remembrance ſooth his mind
With dreams of former days,
When in the lap of Peace reclined
He framed his infant lays;
When Fancy roved at large, nor Care
Nor cold Diſtruſt alarm'd,
Nor Envy with malignant glare
His ſimple youth had harm'd.

RETIREMENT.

'Twas then, O Solitude, to thee
His early vows were paid,
From heart sincere, and warm, and free,
Devoted to the shade.
Ah why did Fate his steps decoy
In stormy paths to roam,
Remote from all congenial joy!—
O take the Wanderer home.

Thy shades, thy silence, now be mine,
Thy charms my only theme;
My haunt the hollow cliff, whose pine
Waves o'er the gloomy stream,
Whence the scared owl on pinions grey
Breaks from the rustling boughs,
And down the lone vale sails away
To more profound repose.

O, while to thee the woodland pours
Its wildly warbling song,
And balmy from the bank of flowers
The zephyr breathes along;
Let no rude sound invade from far,
No vagrant foot be nigh,
No ray from Grandeur's gilded car,
Flash on the startled eye.

But if some pilgrim through the glade
Thy hallow'd bowers explore,
O guard from harm his hoary head
And listen to his lore;
For he of joys divine shall tell
That wean from earthly woe,
And triumph o'er the mighty spell
That chains this heart below.

For me, no more the path invites
Ambition loves to tread;
No more I climb those toilsome heights
By guileful Hope misled;
Leaps my fond fluttering heart no more
To Mirth's enlivening strain;
For present pleasure soon is o'er,
And all the past is vain.

ELEGY.

Written in the year 1758.

STILL shall unthinking man substantial deem
    The forms that fleet through life's deceitful
        dream?
Till at some stroke of Fate the vision flies,
And sad realities in prospect rise;
And, from Elysian slumbers rudely torn,
The startled soul awakes, to think, and mourn.

    O ye, whose hours in jocund train advance,
Whose spirits to the song of gladness dance,
Who flowery plains in endless pomp survey
Glittering in beams of visionary day;
O, yet while Fate delays th' impending woe,
Be roused to thought, anticipate the blow;
Lest, like the lightning's glance, the sudden ill
Flash to confound, and penetrate to kill;
Lest, thus encompass'd with funereal gloom,
Like me, ye bend o'er some untimely tomb,
Pour your wild ravings in Night's frighted ear,
And half pronounce Heaven's sacred doom severe.

ELEGY.

 Wise, Beauteous, Good! O every grace com-
   bined,
That charms the eye, or captivates the mind!
Fresh, as the floweret opening on the morn,
Whose leaves bright drops of liquid pearl adorn!
Sweet, as the downy-pinion'd gale, that roves
To gather fragrance in Arabian groves!
Mild, as the melodies at close of day,
That heard remote along the vale decay!
Yet, why with these compared? What tints so fine,
What sweetness, mildness, can be match'd with thine?
Why roam abroad, since recollection true
Restores the lovely form to Fancy's view?
Still let me gaze, and every care beguile,
Gaze on that cheek, where all the graces smile;
That soul-expressing eye, benignly bright,
Where meekness beams ineffable delight;
That brow, where Wisdom sits enthroned serene,
Each feature forms, and dignifies the mien:
Still let me listen, while her words impart
The sweet effusions of the blameless heart,
Till all my soul, each tumult charm'd away,
Yields, gently led, to Virtue's easy sway.

 By thee inspired, O Virtue, Age is young,
And musick warbles from the faultering tongue:
Thy ray creative cheers the clouded brow,
And decks the faded cheek with rosy glow,

Brightens the joyless aspect, and supplies
Pure heavenly lustre to the languid eyes:
But when Youth's living bloom reflects thy beams,
Resistless on the view the glory streams,
Love, Wonder, Joy, alternately alarm,
And Beauty dazzles with angelic charm.

Ah whither fled! ye dear illusions stay!
Lo, pale and silent lies the lovely clay.
How are the roses on that cheek decay'd,
Which late the purple light of youth display'd!
Health on her form each sprightly grace bestow'd;
With life and thought each speaking feature glow'd.
Fair was the blossom, soft the vernal sky;
Elate with hope we deem'd no tempest nigh;
When lo, a whirlwind's instantaneous gust
Left all its beauties withering in the dust.

Cold the soft hand, that soothed Woe's weary head!
And quench'd the eye, the pitying tear that shed!
And mute the voice, whose pleasing accents stole,
Infusing balm, into the rankled soul!
O Death, why arm with cruelty thy power,
And spare the idle weed, yet lop the flower!
Why fly thy shafts in lawless error driven!
Is Virtue then no more the care of Heaven!

F 4

But peace, bold thought! be still, my bursting heart!
We, not ELIZA, felt the fatal dart.
Escaped the dungeon does the slave complain,
Nor bless the friendly hand that broke the chain?
Say, pines not Virtue for the lingering morn,
On this dark wild condemn'd to roam forlorn?
Where Reason's meteor-rays, with sickly glow,
O'er the dun gloom a dreadful glimmering throw;
Disclosing dubious to th' affrighted eye
O'erwhelming mountains tottering from on high,
Black billowy deeps in storm perpetual toss'd,
And weary ways in wildering labyrinths lost.
O happy stroke, that burst the bonds of clay,
Darts through the rending gloom the blaze of day,
And wings the soul with boundless flight to soar,
Where dangers threat, and fears alarm no more.

 Transporting thought! here let me wipe away
The tear of grief, and wake a bolder lay.
But ah! the swimming eye o'erflows anew;
Nor check the sacred drops to pity due;
Lo, where in speechless, hopeless anguish, bend
O'er her loved dust, the Parent, Brother, Friend!
How vain the hope of man! But cease thy strain,
Nor Sorrow's dread solemnity profane;
Mix'd with yon drooping Mourners, on her bier
In silence shed the sympathetick tear.

ODE

TO

HOPE.

I. 1.

O Thou, who glad'st the pensive soul,
   More than Aurora's smile the swain forlorn,
Left all night long to mourn
Where desolation frowns, and tempests howl;
And shrieks of Woe, as intermits the storm,
Far o'er the monstrous wilderness resound,
And cross the gloom darts many a shapeless form,
And many a fire-eyed visage glares around.
O come, and be once more my guest.
Come, for thou oft thy suppliant's vow hast heard,
And oft with smiles indulgent chear'd
And soothed him into rest.

I. 2.

Smit by thy rapture-beaming eye
Deep flashing through the midnight of their mind,
The sable bands combined,
Where Fear's black banner bloats the troubled sky,

Appall'd retire. Suspicion hides her head,
Nor dares th' obliquely gleaming eyeball raise;
Despair, with gorgon-figured veil o'erspread,
Speeds to dark Phlegethon's detested maze.
Lo, startled at the heavenly ray,
With speed unwonted Indolence upsprings,
And, heaving, lifts her leaden wings,
And sullen glides away:

I. 3.

Ten thousand forms, by pining Fancy view'd,
Dissolve. Above the sparkling flood
When Phebus rears his awful brow,
From lengthening lawn and valley low
The troops of fen-born mists retire.
Along the plain
The joyous swain
Eyes the gay villages again,
And gold-illumined spire;
While on the billowy ether borne
Floats the loose lay's jovial measure;
And light along the fairy Pleasure,
Her green robes glittering to the morn,
Wantons on silken wing. And goblins all
To the damp dungeon shrink, or hoary hall,
Or westward, with impetuous flight,
Shoot to the desart realms of their congenial Night.

ODE TO HOPE.

II. 1.

When first on Childhood's eager gaze
Life's varied landscape, stretch'd immense around,
Starts out of night profound,
Thy voice incites to tempt th' untrodden maze.
Fond he surveys thy mild maternal face,
His bashful eye still kindling as he views,
And, while thy lenient arm supports his pace,
With beating heart the upland path pursues:
The path that leads, where, hung sublime,
And seen afar, youth's gallant trophies, bright
In Fancy's rainbow ray, invite
His wingy nerves to climb.

II. 2.

Pursue thy pleasurable way,
Safe in the guidance of thy heavenly guard,
While melting airs are heard,
And soft-eyed cherub forms around thee play:
Simplicity, in careless flowers array'd,
Prattling amusive in his accent meek;
And Modesty, half turning as afraid,
The smile just dimpling on his glowing cheek;
Content and Leisure, hand in hand
With Innocence and Peace, advance, and sing;
And Mirth, in many a mazy ring,
Frisks o'er the flowery land.

II. 3.

Frail man, how various is thy lot below!
To-day though gales propitious blow,
And Peace soft gliding down the sky
Lead Love along and Harmony,
To-morrow the gay scene deforms:
Then all around
The thunder's found
Rolls rattling on through heaven's profound,
And down rush all the storms.
Ye days, that balmy influence shed,
When sweet Childhood, ever sprightly,
In paths of pleasure sported lightly,
Whither, ah whither are ye fled!
Ye cherub train, that brought him on his way,
O leave him not midst tumult and dismay;
For now youth's eminence he gains:
But what a weary length of lingering toil remains!

III. 1.

They shrink, they vanish into air.
Now Slander taints with pestilence the gale;
And mingling cries assail,
The wail of Woe, and groan of grim Despair.
Lo, wizard Envy from his serpent eye
Darts quick destruction in each baleful glance;

ODE TO HOPE.

Pride smiling stern, and yellow Jealousy,
Frowning Disdain, and haggard Hate advance;
Behold, amidst the dire array,
Pale wither'd Care his giant-stature rears,
And lo, his iron hand prepares
To grasp its feeble prey.

III. 2.

Who now will guard bewilder'd youth
Safe from the fierce assault of hostile rage?
Such war can Virtue wage,
Virtue, that bears the sacred shield of Truth?
Alas! full oft on Guilt's victorious car
The spoils of Virtue are in triumph borne;
While the fair captive, mark'd with many a scar,
In lone obscurity, oppress'd, forlorn,
Resigns to tears her angel form.
Ill-fated youth, then whither wilt thou fly?
No friend, no shelter now is nigh,
And onwards rolls the storm.

III. 3.

But whence the sudden beam that shoots along?
Why shrink aghast the hostile throng?
Lo, from amidst affliction's night,
Hope bursts all radiant on the sight:
Her words the troubled bosom sooth.

" Why thus dismay'd?
" Though foes invade,
" Hope ne'er is wanting to their aid,
" Who tread the path of truth.
" 'Tis I, who smooth the rugged way,
" I, who close the eyes of Sorrow,
" And with glad visions of to-morrow
" Repair the weary soul's decay.
" When Death's cold touch thrills to the freezing
      " heart,
" Dreams of heaven's opening glories I impart,
" Till the freed spirit springs on high
" In rapture too severe for weak Mortality."

PYGMÆO-GERANO-MACHIA,

THE BATTLE OF

THE PYGMIES AND CRANES.

From the Latin of ADDISON.

1762.

THE pygmy-people, and the feather'd train,
  Mingling in mortal combat on the plain,
I sing. Ye Muses, favour my designs,
Lead on my squadrons, and arrange the lines;
The flashing swords and fluttering wings display,
And long bills nibbling in the bloody fray;
Cranes darting with disdain on tiny foes,
Conflicting birds and men, and war's unnumber'd
  woes.

 The wars and woes of heroes six feet long
Have oft resounded in Pierian song.
Who has not heard of Colchos' golden fleece,
And Argo mann'd with all the flower of Greece?
Of Thebes' fell brethren, Theseus stern of face,
And Peleus' son unrival'd in the race,
Eneas founder of the Roman line,
And William glorious on the banks of Boyne?

Who has not learn'd to weep at Pompey's woes,
And over Blackmore's Epic page to doze?
'Tis I, who dare attempt unusual strains,
Of hosts unsung, and unfrequented plains;
The small shrill trump, and chiefs of little size,
And armies rushing down the darken'd skies.

Where India reddens to the early dawn,
Winds a deep vale from vulgar eye withdrawn:
Bosom'd in groves the lowly region lies,
And rocky mountains round the border rise.
Here, till the doom of fate its fall decreed,
The empire flourish'd of the pygmy-breed;
Here Industry perform'd, and Genius plan'd,
And busy multitudes o'erspread the land.
But now to these lone bounds if pilgrim stray,
Tempting through craggy cliffs the desperate way,
He finds the puny mansion fallen to earth,
Its godlings mouldering on th' abandon'd hearth;
And starts, where small white bones are spread around,
" Or little footsteps lightly print the ground;"
While the proud crane her nest securely builds,
Chattering amid the desolated fields.

But different fates befel her hostile rage,
While reign'd, invincible through many an age,
The dreaded Pygmy: rouſed by war's alarms
Forth rush'd the madding Mannikin to arms.

Fierce to the field of death the hero flies;
The faint crane fluttering flaps the ground, and
    dies;
And by the victor borne (o'erwhelming load!)
With bloody bill loose-dangling marks the road.
And oft the wily dwarf in ambush lay,
And often made the callow young his prey;
With slaughter'd victims heap'd his board, and
    smiled
T' avenge the parent's trespass on the child.
Oft, where his feather'd foe had rear'd her nest,
And laid her eggs and houshold gods to rest,
Burning for blood, in terrible array,
The eighteen-inch militia burst their way:
All went to wreck; the infant foeman fell,
When scarce his chirping bill had broke the shell.

  Loud uproar hence, and rage of arms arose,
And the fell rancour of encountering foes;
Hence dwarfs and cranes one general havock whelms,
And Death's grim visage scares the pygmy-realms.
Not half so furious blazed the warlike fire
Of Mice, high theme of the Meonian lyre;
When bold to battle march'd th' accouter'd frogs,
And the deep tumult thunder'd through the bogs.
Pierced by the javelin-bulrush on the shore
Here agonizing roll'd the mouse in gore;

G

And there the frog (a scene full sad to see!)
Shorn of one leg slow sprawl'd along on three:
He vaults no more with vigorous hops on high,
But mourns in hoarsest croaks his destiny.

And now the day of woe drew on apace,
A day of woe to all the pygmy-race,
When dwarfs were doom'd (but penitence was vain)
To rue each broken egg, and chicken slain.
For roused to vengeance by repeated wrong
From distant climes the long-bill'd legions throng:
From Strymon's lake, Cäyster's plashy meads,
And fens of Scythia green with rustling reeds;
From where the Danube winds through many a land,
And Mareotis laves th' Egyptian strand,
To rendezvous they waft on eager wing,
And wait assembled the returning spring.
Meanwhile they trim their plumes for length of flight,
Whet their keen beaks, and twisting claws, for fight;
Each crane the pygmy power in thought o'erturns,
And every bosom for the battle burns.

When genial gales the frozen air unbind,
The screaming legions wheel, and mount the wind.
Far in the sky they form their long array,
And land and ocean stretch'd immense survey

Deep deep beneath; and, triumphing in pride,
With clouds and winds commix'd, innumerous ride;
'Tis wild obstreperous clangour all, and heaven
Whirls, in tempestuous undulation driven.

Nor less th' alarm that shook the world below,
Where march'd in pomp of war th' embattled foe;
Where mannikins with haughty step advance,
And grasp the shield, and couch the quivering lance;
To right and left the lengthening lines they form,
And rank'd in deep array await the storm.

High in the midst the chieftain-dwarf was seen,
Of giant stature, and imperial mien.
Full twenty inches tall he strode along,
And view'd with lofty eye the wondering throng;
And, while with many a scar his visage frown'd,
Bared his broad bosom rough with many a wound
Of beaks and claws, disclosing to their sight
The glorious meed of high heroick might.
For with insatiate vengeance, he pursued,
And never-ending hate, the feathery brood.
Unhappy they, confiding in the length
Of horny beak, or talon's crooked strength,
Who durst abide his rage; the blade descends,
And from the panting trunk the pinion rends.

Laid low in duſt the pinion waves no more,
The trunk disfigured ſtiffens in its gore.
What hoſts of heroes fell beneath his force!
What heaps of chicken carnage mark'd his courſe!
How oft, O Strymon, thy lone banks along,
Did wailing echo waft the funeral ſong!

And now from far the mingling clamours riſe,
Loud and more loud rebounding through the ſkies.
From ſkirt to ſkirt of heaven, with ſtormy ſway,
A cloud rolls on, and darkens all the day.
Near and more near deſcends the dreadful ſhade:
And now in battailous array diſplay'd,
On ſounding wings, and ſcreaming in their ire,
The cranes ruſh onward, and the fight require.

The pygmy warriors eye with fearleſs glare
The hoſt thick ſwarming o'er the burthen'd air;
Thick ſwarming now, but to their native land
Doom'd to return a ſcanty ſtraggling band.
When ſudden, darting down the depth of heaven,
Fierce on th' expecting foe the cranes are driven.
The kindling phrenſy every boſom warms,
The region echoes to the craſh of arms:
Looſe feathers from the encountering armies fly,
And in careering whirlwinds mount the ſky.

THE PYGMIES AND CRANES.

To breathe from toil upsprings the panting crane,
Then with fresh vigour downwards darts again.
Success in equal balance hovering hangs.
Here, on the sharp spear, mad with mortal pangs,
The bird transfix'd in bloody vortex whirls,
Yet fierce in death the threatening talon curls:
There, while the life-blood bubbles from his wound,
With little feet the pygmy beats the ground;
Deep from his breast the short short sob he draws,
And dying curses the keen-pointed claws.
Trembles the thundering field, thick cover'd o'er
With falchions, mangled wings, and streaming gore,
And pygmy arms, and beaks of ample size;
And here a claw, and there a finger lies.

 Encompass'd round with heaps of slaughter'd foes,
All grim in blood the pygmy champion glows.
And on th' assailing host impetuous springs,
Careless of nibbling bills, and flapping wings;
And midst the tumult wheresoe'er he turns,
The battle with redoubled fury burns;
From every side th' avenging cranes amain
Throng, to o'erwhelm this terror of the plain.
When suddenly (for such the will of Jove)
A fowl enormous, sousing from above,
The gallant chieftain clutch'd, and, soaring high,
(Sad chance of battle!) bore him up the sky.

The cranes purſue, and, cluſtering in a ring,
Chatter triumphant round the captive king.
But ah! what pangs each pygmy boſom wrung,
When, now to cranes a prey, on talons hung,
High in the clouds they ſaw their helpleſs lord,
His wriggling form ſtill leſſening as he ſoar'd.

    Lo yet again with unabated rage
In mortal ſtrife the mingling hoſts engage.
The crane with darted bill aſſaults the foe,
Hovering; then wheels aloft to ſcape the blow:
The dwarf in anguiſh aims the vengeful wound;
But whirls in empty air the falchion round.

    Such was the ſcene, when midſt the loud alarms
Sublime th' eternal Thunderer roſe in arms.
When Briareus, by mad ambition driven,
Heaved Pelion huge, and hurl'd it high at heaven.
Jove roll'd redoubling thunders from on high,
Mountains and bolts encounter'd in the ſky;
Till one ſtupendous ruin whelm'd the crew,
  Their vaſt limbs weltering wide in brimſtone
      blue.

    But now at length the pygmy legions yield,
And wing'd with terror fly the flatal field.

THE PYGMIES AND CRANES.

They raise a weak and melancholy wail,
All in distraction scattering o'er the vale.
Prone on their routed rear the cranes descend;
Their bills bite furious, and their talons rend:
With unrelenting ire they urge the chace,
Sworn to exterminate the hated race.

'Twas thus the Pygmy Name, once great in war,
For spoils of conquer'd cranes renown'd afar,
Perish'd. For, by the dread decree of heaven,
Short is the date to earthly grandeur given,
And vain are all attempts to roam beyond
Where Fate has fix'd the everlasting bound.
Fallen are the trophies of Assyrian power,
And Persia's proud dominion is no more;
Yea, though to both superior far in fame,
Thine empire, Latium, is an empty name.

And now with lofty chiefs of ancient time
The pygmy heroes roam th' Elysian clime.
Or, if belief to matron-tales be due,
Full oft, in the belated shepherd's view,
Their frisking forms, in gentle green array'd,
Gambol secure amid the moonlight glade.
Secure, for no alarming cranes molest,
And all their woes in long oblivion rest,

Down the deep dale, and narrow winding way,
They foot it featly, ranged in ringlets gay:
'Tis joy and frolick all, where'er they rove,
And Fairy-people is the name they love.

THE HARES,

A FABLE.

YES, yes, I grant the sons of earth
    Are doom'd to trouble from their birth.
We all of sorrow have our share;
But say, is yours without compare?
Look round the world; perhaps you'll find
Each individual of our kind
Press'd with an equal load of ill,
Equal at least. Look further still,
And own your lamentable case
Is little short of happiness.
In yonder hut that stands alone
Attend to Famine's feeble moan;
Or view the couch where Sickness lies,
Mark his pale cheek, and languid eyes,
His frame by strong convulsion torn,
His struggling sighs, and looks forlorn.
Or see, transfix'd with keener pangs,
Where o'er his hoard the miser hangs;

THE HARES,

Whistles the wind; he starts, he stares,
Nor Slumber's balmy blessing shares;
Despair, Remorse, and Terror roll
Their tempests on his harass'd soul.

But here perhaps it may avail
T' enforce our reasoning with a tale.

Mild was the morn, the sky serene,
The jolly hunting band convene,
The beagle's breast with ardour burns,
The bounding steed the champaign spurns,
And Fancy oft the game descries
Through the hound's nose, and huntsman's eyes.

Just then, a council of the hares
Had met, on national affairs.
The chiefs were set; while o'er their head
The furze its frizzled covering spread.
Long lists of grievances were heard,
And general discontent appear'd.
" Our harmless race shall every savage
" Both quadruped and biped ravage?
" Shall horses, hounds, and hunters still
" Unite their wits to work us ill?
" The youth, his parent's sole delight,
" Whose tooth the dewy lawns invite,

" Whose pulse in every vein beats strong,
" Whose limbs leap light the vales along,
" May yet ere noontide meet his death,
" And lie dismember'd on the heath.
" For youth, alas, nor cautious age,
" Nor strength, nor speed, eludes their rage.
" In every field we meet the foe,
" Each gale comes fraught with sounds of woe;
" The morning but awakes our fears,
" The evening sees us bathed in tears.
" But must we ever idly grieve,
" Nor strive our fortunes to relieve?
" Small is each individual's force:
" To stratagem be our recourse;
" And then, from all our tribes combined,
" The murderer to his coast may find
" No foes are weak, whom Justice arms,
" Whom Concord leads, and Hatred warms.
" Be roused; or liberty acquire,
" Or in the great attempt expire."
He said no more, for in his breast
Conflicting thoughts the voice suppress'd;
The fire of vengeance seem'd to stream
From his swoln eyeball's yellow gleam.

 And now the tumults of the war,
Mingling confusedly from afar,

Swell in the wind.   Now louder cries
Diſtinct of hounds and men ariſe.
Forth from the brake, with beating heart,
Th' aſſembled hares tumultuous ſtart,
And, every ſtraining nerve on wing,
Away precipitately ſpring.
The hunting band, a ſignal given,
Thick thundering o'er the plain are driven;
O'er cliff abrupt, and ſhrubby mound,
And river broad, impetuous bound;
Now plunge amid the foreſt ſhades,
Glance through the openings of the glades;
Now o'er the level valley ſweep,
Now with ſhort ſteps ſtrain up the ſteep;
While backward from the hunter's eyes
The landſcape like a torrent flies.
At laſt an antient wood they gain'd,
By pruner's ax yet unprofaned.
High o'er the reſt, by Nature rear'd,
The oak's majeſtick boughs appear'd;
Beneath, a copſe of various hue
In barbarous luxuriance grew.
No knife had curb'd the rambling ſprays,
No hand had wove th' implicit maze.
The flowering thorn, ſelf-taught to wind,
The hazle's ſtubborn ſtem intwined,
And bramble twigs were wreath'd around,
And rough furze crept along the ground.

A FABLE.

Here sheltering, from the sons of murther,
The hares drag their tired limbs no further.

But lo, the western wind erelong
Was loud, and roar'd the woods among;
From rustling leaves, and crashing boughs,
The sound of woe and war arose.
The hares distracted scour the grove,
As terror and amazement drove;
But danger, wheresoe'er they fled,
Still seem'd impending o'er their head.
Now crowded in a grotto's gloom,
All hope extinct, they wait their doom.
Dire was the silence, till, at length,
Even from despair deriving strength,
With bloody eye, and furious look,
A daring youth arose, and spoke.

" O wretched race, the scorn of Fate,
" Whom ills of every sort await!
" O, cursed with keenest sense to feel
" The sharpest sting of every ill!
" Say ye, who, fraught with mighty scheme,
" Of liberty and vengeance dream,
" What now remains? To what recess
" Shall we our weary steps address,
" Since fate is evermore pursuing
" All ways and means to work our ruin?

THE HARES,

"Are we alone, of all beneath,
"Condemn'd to misery worse than death!
"Must we, with fruitless labour, strive
"In misery worse than death to live!
"No. Be the smaller ill our choice:
"So dictates Nature's powerful voice.
"Death's pang will in a moment cease;
"And then, All hail, eternal peace!"
Thus while he spoke, his words impart
The dire resolve to every heart.

A distant lake in prospect lay,
That glittering in the solar ray,
Gleam'd through the dusky trees, and shot
A trembling light along the grot.
Thither with one consent they bend,
Their sorrows with their lives to end,
While each, in thought, already hears
The water hissing in his ears.

Fast by the margin of the lake,
Conceal'd within a thorny brake,
A Linnet sate, whose careless lay
Amused the solitary day.
Careless he sung, for on his breast
Sorrow no lasting trace impress'd;
When suddenly he heard a sound
Of swift feet traversing the ground.

A FABLE.

Quick to the neighbouring tree he flies,
Thence trembling casts around his eyes;
No foe appear'd, his fears were vain;
Pleased he renews the sprightly strain,

The hares, whose noise had caused his fright,
Saw with surprise the linnet's flight.
Is there on earth a wretch, they said,
Whom our approach can strike with dread?
An instantaneous change of thought
To tumult every bosom wrought.
So fares the system-building sage,
Who, plodding on from youth to age,
At last on some foundation-dream
Has rear'd aloft his goodly scheme,
And proved his predecessors fools,
And bound all nature by his rules;
So fares he in that dreadful hour,
When injured Truth exerts her power,
Some new phenomenon to raise;
Which, bursting on his frighted gaze,
From its proud summit to the ground
Proves the whole edifice unsound.

" Children," thus spoke a hare sedate,
Who oft had known th' extremes of fate,
" In flight events the docile mind
" May hints of good instruction find.

" That our condition is the worst,
" And we with such misfortunes cursed
" As all comparison defy,
" Was late the universal cry.
" When lo, an accident so slight
" As yonder little linnet's flight
" Has made your stubborn heart confess
" (So your amazement bids me guess)
" That all our load of woes and fears
" Is but a part of what he bears.
" Where can he rest secure from harms,
" Whom even a helpless hare alarms?
" Yet he repines not at his lot,
" When past the danger is forgot:
" On yonder bough he trims his wings,
" And with unusual rapture sings;
" While we, less wretched, sink beneath
" Our lighter ills, and rush to death.
" No more of this unmeaning rage,
" But hear, my friends, the words of age.

" When by the winds of autumn driven
" The scatter'd clouds fly cross the heaven,
" Oft have we, from some mountain's head,
" Beheld th' alternate light and shade
" Sweep the long vale. Here hovering lowers
" The shadowy cloud; there downwards pours,

A FABLE.

"Streaming direct, a flood of day,
"Which from the view flies swift away;
"It flies, while other shades advance,
"And other streaks of sunshine glance.
"Thus chequer'd is the life below
"With gleams of joy, and clouds of woe.
"Then hope not, while we journey on,
"Still to be basking in the sun:
"Nor fear, though now in shades ye mourn,
"That sunshine will no more return.
"If, by your terrors overcome,
"Ye fly before th' approaching gloom,
"The rapid clouds your flight pursue,
"And darkness still o'ercasts your view.
"Who longs to reach the radiant plain
"Must onward urge his course amain;
"For doubly swift the shadow flies,
"When 'gainst the gale the pilgrim plies.
"At least be firm, and undismay'd
"Maintain your ground; the fleeting shade
"Erelong spontaneous glides away,
"And gives you back th' enlivening ray.
"Lo, while I speak; our danger past!
"No more the shrill horn's angry blast
"Howls in our ear; the savage roar
"Of war and murder is no more.
"Then snatch the moment fate allows,
"Nor think of past or future woes."

He spoke; and hope revives; the lake
That instant one and all forsake,
In sweet amusement to employ
The present sprightly hour of joy.

 Now from the western mountain's brow
Compass'd with clouds of various glow,
The sun a broader orb displays,
And shoots aslope his ruddy rays.
The lawn assumes a fresher green,
And dew-drops spangle all the scene.
The balmy zephyr breathes along,
The shepherd sings his tender song,
With all their lays the groves resound,
And falling waters murmur round.
Discord and care were put to flight,
And all was peace, and calm delight.

EPITAPH:

Being part of an Inscription for a Monument to be erected by a Gentleman to the Memory of his Lady.

FAREWELL, my best-beloved; whose heavenly mind
Genius with virtue, strength with softness join'd;
Devotion, undebased by pride or art,
With meek simplicity, and joy of heart;
Though sprightly, gentle; though polite, sincere;
And only of thyself a judge severe;
Unblamed, unequal'd, in each sphere of life,
The tenderest Daughter, Sister, Parent, Wife.
In thee their Patroness th' afflicted lost;
Thy friends, their pattern, ornament, and boast;
And I—but ah, can words my loss declare,
Or paint th' extremes of transport and despair!
O Thou, beyond what verse or speech can tell,
My guide, my friend, my best-beloved, farewell!

O D E

ON

LORD H**'s BIRTH-DAY.

A MUSE, unskill'd in venal praise,
Unstain'd with flattery's art;
Who loves simplicity of lays
Breathed ardent from the heart;
While gratitude and joy inspire,
Resumes the long-unpractised lyre,
To hail, O H**, thy Natal Morn:
No gaudy wreathe of flowers she weaves,
But twines with oak the laurel leaves,
Thy cradle to adorn.

For not on beds of gaudy flowers
Thine ancestors reclined,
Where Sloth dissolves, and Spleen devours
All energy of mind.

ODE ON LORD H**'s BIRTH-DAY.

To hurl the dart, to ride the car,
To stem the deluges of war,
And snatch from fate a sinking land;
Trample th' Invader's lofty crest,
And from his grasp the dagger wrest,
And desolating brand:

'Twas this, that raised th' illustrious Line
To match the first in fame;
A thousand years have seen it shine
With unabated flame.
Have seen thy mighty Sires appear
Foremost in Glory's high career,
The pride and pattern of the Brave.
Yet, pure from lust of blood their fire,
And from Ambition's wild desire,
They triumph'd but to save.

The Muse with joy attends their way
The vale of peace along;
There to its Lord the village gay
Renews the grateful song.
Yon castle's glittering towers contain
No pit of woe, nor clanking chain,
Nor to the suppliant's wail resound;
The open doors the needy bless,
Th' unfriended hail their calm recess,
And gladness smiles around.

There to the sympathetick heart
Life's best delights belong,
To mitigate the mourner's smart,
To guard the weak from wrong.
Ye Sons of Luxury, be wise;
Know, happiness for ever flies
The cold and solitary breast;
Then let the social instinct glow,
And learn to feel another's woe,
And in his joy be bless'd.

O yet, ere Pleasure plant her snare
For unsuspecting youth;
Ere Flattery her song prepare
To check the voice of Truth;
O may his country's guardian-Power
Attend the slumbering Infant's bower,
And bright, inspiring dreams impart;
To rouse th' hereditary fire,
To kindle each sublime desire,
Exalt, and warm the heart.

Swift to reward a Parent's fears,
A Parent's hopes to crown,
Roll on in peace, ye blooming years,
That rear him to renown;

ODE ON LORD H**'s BIRTH-DAY.

When in his finish'd form and face
Admiring multitudes shall trace
Each patrimonial charm combined,
The courteous yet majestick mien,
The liberal smile, the look serene,
The great and gentle mind.

Yet, though thou draw a nation's eyes,
And win a nation's love,
Let not thy towering mind despise
The village and the grove.
No slander there shall wound thy fame,
No ruffian take his deadly aim,
No rival weave the secret snare:
For Innocence with angel smile,
Simplicity that knows not guile,
And Love and Peace are there.

When winds the mountain oak assail,
And lay its glories waste,
Content may slumber in the vale,
Unconscious of the blast.
Through scenes of tumult while we roam,
The heart, alas! is ne'er at home,
It hopes in time to roam no more;
The mariner, not vainly brave,
Combats the storm, and rides the wave,
To rest at last on shore.

ODE ON LORD H**'s BIRTH-DAY.

Ye proud, ye selfish, ye severe,
How vain your mask of state!
The good alone have joy sincere,
The good alone are great:
Great, when, amid the vale of peace,
They bid the plaint of sorrow cease,
And hear the voice of artless praise;
As when along the trophy'd plain
Sublime they lead the victor train,
While shouting nations gaze.

THE HERMIT.

AT the close of the day, when the hamlet is still,
And mortals the sweets of forgetfulness prove,
When nought but the torrent is heard on the hill,
And nought but the nightingale's song in the grove:
'Twas thus, by the cave of the mountain afar,
While his harp rung symphonious, a Hermit began;
No more with himself or with nature at war,
He thought as a Sage, though he felt as a Man.

" Ah why, all abandon'd to darkness and woe,
" Why, lone Philomela, that languishing fall?
" For Spring shall return, and a lover bestow,
" And Sorrow no longer thy bosom inthral.
" But, if pity inspire thee, renew the sad lay,
" Mourn, sweetest complainer, man calls thee to
    " mourn;
" O soothe him, whose pleasures like thine pass
    " away.
" Full quickly they pass—but they never return.

THE HERMIT.

" Now gliding remote, on the verge of the sky,
" The Moon half extinguish'd her crescent displays:
" But lately I mark'd, when majestick on high
" She shone, and the planets were lost in her blaze.
" Roll on, thou fair orb, and with gladness pursue
" The path that conducts thee to splendor again.
" But Man's faded glory what change shall renew!
" Ah fool! to exult in a glory so vain!

" 'Tis night, and the landscape is lovely no more;
" I mourn, but, ye woodlands, I mourn not for you;
" For morn is approaching, your charms to restore,
" Perfumed with fresh fragrance, and glittering with
    " dew.
" Nor yet for the ravage of winter I mourn;
" Kind Nature the embryo blossom will save.
" But when shall Spring visit the mouldering urn!
" O when shall it dawn on the night of the grave!"

' 'Twas thus, by the glare of false Science betray'd,
' That leads, to bewilder; and dazzles, to blind;
' My thoughts wont to roam, from shade onward to
    ' shade,
' Destruction before me, and sorrow behind.
" O pity, great Father of light," then I cry'd,
" Thy creature who fain would not wander from Thee!
" Lo, humbled in dust, I relinquish my pride:
' From doubt and from darkness thou only canst free."

THE HERMIT.

' And darkneſs and doubt are now flying away.
' No longer I roam in conjecture forlorn.
' So breaks on the traveller, faint, and aſtray,
' The bright and the balmy effulgence of morn.
' See Truth, Love, and Mercy, in triumph de-
  ' ſcending,
' And Nature all glowing in Eden's firſt bloom!
' On the cold cheek of Death ſmiles and roſes are
  ' blending,
' And Beauty Immortal awakes from the tomb.'

THE END.